GHOSTS AND LEGENDS OF YONKERS

JASON MEDINA

Haunted America

Published by Haunted America
A Division of The History Press
Charleston, SC 29403
www.historypress.net

Copyright © 2015 by Jason Medina of Tribal Publications, Inc.
All rights reserved

Back cover, top: Boyce Thompson Institute. *Courtesy of the Yonkers Historical Society*; *inset*: Pavilion
at Untermyer Park. *Photo by Xavier Gonzalez.*

Unless otherwise noted, all images appear courtesy of the author.

First published 2015

Manufactured in the United States

ISBN 978.1.62619.519.6

Library of Congress control number: 2015945066

Tribe.

CONTENTS

ACKNOWLEDGEMENTS

I have so many people to thank for making this book possible. I will begin with my team, Yonkers Ghost Investigators. Some members grew up in Yonkers and are longtime residents, while a few moved away. There are also members who have never resided in Yonkers but still took the time to do investigations here. Many teammates have gone with me to some of these locations to verify if there was any truth to the rumors we've heard or read about.

First is my beautiful wife, Jo-Ann Santos-Medina, the team's first senior field investigator. She helps me in so many ways in regard to research and investigations, by going over hours of evidence and by helping to proofread my books. She's gone with me on more investigations than any other member to date. Many of those investigations were conducted in Yonkers.

Next, I'd like to thank my former co-team leader and founding member, my cousin Christina Claudio. She was the only one with me during the team's initial paranormal investigation on November 25, 2006. On that groundbreaking night, we were lucky enough to acquire our first photo of an apparition at Saint Joseph's Cemetery in Yonkers.

My second senior field investigator and nephew, Chris Gonzalez, is next on my list. He was with me in 2006 on the team's third paranormal investigation when we got our third photo of an apparition. We were at Oakland Cemetery in Yonkers. Chris has been on the team longer than anyone else, aside from myself. He shared his personal experiences regarding his former residence, which is included in this book.

Former senior field investigators Giselle Hernandez and my cousins Jonathan and Meagan Morales, along with Tatiana Morales, have joined me on several investigations at a couple cemeteries in Yonkers. Meagan was actually at Saint Joseph's Cemetery with Christina and I during our second investigation when we captured one of our best apparition photos to date. It was only our second investigation, and we already managed to obtain our "Holy Grail" of evidence.

Incidentally, the photos I've mentioned are in this book.

Thank you to our former website manager, Melissa Mezo. It was because of her insistence that we have a website today. She was the one who created our first website and had the brilliant idea to add the name "Yonkers" to the front of our team's name. Until then, we just called ourselves "Ghost Investigators." It was only a hobby, so we thought nothing of it. While on the team, Melissa was also instrumental in capturing excellent electronic voice phenomena (EVP) recordings at Saint Joseph's Cemetery. After her amicable departure from the team, I created the current website from scratch and added pages to both Myspace and Facebook.

My technical crew chief, Xavier Gonzalez, has proven to be extremely helpful on investigations in and outside of Yonkers. It pains me to say I almost denied him membership to the team because I believed we had more than enough members at the time. We remained friends, regardless of this near fatal error on my part. In time, I saw the potential he had and quickly changed my mind. I'm extremely grateful to have him on the team. He's become a special part of our team and his photography skills have been an invaluable asset. He was even the photographer at my wedding. Needless to say, we are the best of friends.

Thanks to my other technical crewmembers, Richard Embree and my cousin Reuven Levy. They've both taken part on investigations in and outside of Yonkers. I'm glad to have them on the team. Coincidentally, I almost denied Rich entry onto the team for the very same reason I denied Xavier. Once again, I realized I was making a mistake. It's a good thing, too, because Rich has been a tremendous help with researching locations for this book and with setting up video cameras during our investigations. Like with Xavier, we also became great friends.

Actually, my team members are like an extended family to me. For that reason, I am very careful whom I recruit and allow into our close-knit circle. I don't ever recruit complete strangers, although we get a lot of requests to join.

Other current teammates who have participated on investigations within the confines of Yonkers are my cousin Sarah Morales and our friends

Andrew Ramnanan, Devin Larkin and Sam Bartels and one of our newest members, Kelly Seufert. Thank you all so much for helping out and doing your part.

I would like to take a moment to extend thanks to some of our former team members, who took part in some of our Yonkers investigations. A few were significant in gathering the information used in this book. Thank you very much to Natasha Brockington, Olivia Brockington, Amanda Velazquez, Kimberly Warek, Jason Bennett, Jessica Rivera, Amy Martinez and Barbara Gonzalez.

That covers my team's current and past members, in regard to our Yonkers investigations. It's time for me to thank those who helped out in other ways.

Let me begin with Whitney Landis of The History Press. It is thanks to her interest in my team's website that I was selected to write this book. She sought me out to write it. It wasn't the other way around. I was so honored, considering I was barely done with my first novel at the time. She was extremely patient while I finished with my other book projects and did not rush me to start this book. If not for her, this book may not even exist, or she might have found someone else to write it. Not to sound full of myself, but I believe I was the right person for the job, based on my dedication when it comes to doing a thorough research job, my experience with haunted locations in Yonkers, my connection to the Yonkers Historical Society and the fact that I simply love to write. Thank you, Whitney. You are an awesome person. If only all writers could have the pleasure of dealing with someone as patient and kind as you, but then you would not be as unique as you are now.

Of course, I definitely have to thank my helpful friends and fellow members of the Yonkers Historical Society for allowing me to enter their group and taking the time to assist me with research, while giving me input based on their historical knowledge and experiences, not to mention allowing me access to their extensive photo collection. There are so many to thank, but I can only name a few. Thank you to Mary Hoar, Margaret Vitulli, Joan Jennings, Peggy Murphy, Mina Crasson, Angelique Piwinski, Andrew Romano, Deirdre Rylander and, of course, Jerry Ostroff. Thanks for volunteering to help proofread this book, Jerry!

When I joined the Yonkers Historical Society, I dragged my new wife into it with me. We both became volunteers at the historic Sherwood House, the oldest farmhouse in Yonkers and the second-oldest house in Yonkers, second to Philipse Manor Hall. It was also home to Yonkers' first doctor. Within a few months, we were both admitted into the Archive Committee, which is an incredible honor. I was even named the Volunteer of the Year for 2014, which was by far the greatest honor ever bestowed on me. It gave me a chance to shake hands and take photos with the Honorable Mayor Mike Spano. Thanks for attending my awards ceremony and for being both friendly and approachable. You are a true gentleman.

Special thanks to the staff at the Grinton I. Will Branch of the Yonkers Public Library for allowing me to spend hours of research time undisturbed at my favorite table near the window, while going over the many books for the reference material I required.

In addition, I'd like to thank the staff of Philipse Manor Hall and the Hudson River Museum. My visits to both locations were enjoyable and educational. I was able to learn a great deal about Yonkers history just by reading the historic poster boards on display throughout the Manor Hall. I also learned a great deal from the exhibits at both museums.

Thanks to those who were willing to share personal stories and photos with me, such as Donna Parish-Bischoff, Mike Matessino, Jason Savitt, Robert Yasinsac, John Tantillo, Alex Vanino, Kirk F. Myers and Al Romano. Also, a huge thanks to the people on Facebook who have helped me out and supported me by buying my books. There are so many to name, it would take another page.

Last but not least, there are my parents, Waldemar and Mildred Medina, my other proofreaders. Thanks for making the move with me to Yonkers back in 2000. It was a big step for us, but it was worth it for me, as you can see. My life has improved tenfold from what it was before, while living in the Bronx. Thanks for helping me whenever I needed you and for supporting me in everything I do. Most of all, thanks for having me all those years ago and for being great parents. You've helped make me into the man I am today. I know you are proud of me for the things I've accomplished in my life up to this point. I hope you will continue to be with every new thing I do from this moment on because I'm not done, yet. I love you both.

OK, now that we've gotten all the mushy stuff out of the way, let's move on to the introduction!

INTRODUCTION

Located at the southern tip of Westchester County, Yonkers is the closest city in the county to New York City and therefore serves as the gateway between New York City and the Hudson River Valley. There are five major highways connecting it to New York City and the rest of Westchester County. In addition, it has ten Metro North Railroad stations. Yonkers is approximately twenty-one square miles in size, making it one of the largest cities in the state. Founded in 1646 by Adriaen Cornelissen van der Donck, it was named for his property, "Colen Donck," which was called "Jonkheer's Landt," or the land of the young lord.

Naturally, being such an old city makes it ideal for having its fair share of ghost stories and strange legends. While researching for this book, I learned of quite a few interesting stories. Sadly, there were so many that I wasn't able to fit them all. It turns out there are many haunted locations in Yonkers.

All it takes is for one wayward spirit to hold on to his or her past life for a haunting to take place. It is unfortunate when a spirit cannot accept death and feels the need to linger in a state of virtual nonexistence. Sometimes spirits are not aware they are dead, while other times they refuse to "go into the light."

As a paranormal investigator, my main goal has always been to prove the existence of ghosts. I won't call it life after death, since it's really no kind of life. It's only an existence, which is very different from our own. No one can truly say what it's like, since dead people can't write books to tell about it. We can merely take the word of people that have had near-death experiences or learn by analyzing EVP recordings or even with help from mediums.

I first became interested in ghosts while growing up in the Bronx. I was born and raised in the Bronx. I lived in a three-family private house on Ryer Avenue until my late twenties. My parents and I were on the second floor. My aunt and cousins lived on the first floor, while my grandparents lived on the third floor. Other family members came and went throughout the many years we lived there.

When I was about six or seven years old, two of my older cousins used to tell me about a young girl who died in our house on the third floor. She had been very sick. I don't know if they told me to scare me or just to share the information with me. Whatever the case, I became fascinated by the possibility that the ghost of this young girl could manifest to me at any moment. She never did, but whenever the door slammed shut, I would say she wanted the door closed. Of course, my bedroom had a nice draft coming from the window. The bottom line is I was never afraid of her or of any ghost afterward.

During my youth, I spent a good many years going to Yonkers. At first, it was to visit my cousins on Caryl Avenue, where I'd sometimes stay over for the weekend or for an entire week during the summer months. Aside from the time I spent with family, there was something I liked about being in Yonkers that felt different from the Bronx. The suburban life appealed to me. I liked the idea of seeing trees everywhere.

As I got older, I learned to drive. When I bought my first car, a black 1987 Chevy Cavalier, Yonkers was my first destination. I eventually began dating a girl from Yonkers, who lived right around the corner from my cousins. I started shopping along Central Park Avenue on a weekly basis with my brother, my parents, my cousins or my girlfriend at the time. My brother and I still go to Central Park Avenue each week. It's become our bonding ritual. I also shop there often with my wife.

The extra time I spent in Yonkers gave me more reasons to experience what the city had to offer, and I came to enjoy it immensely. I loved Yonkers and Westchester County mainly for their beauty, serenity and conveniences. When I began looking for a place to move, I tried to focus my search in Yonkers or in Lower Westchester County. In the end, I told my real estate agent, Alfredo Rivera, to find me a house in Yonkers, and he did.

By the end of 2000, I bought a house on Nepperhan Avenue together with my father. It was a great place for a new start. Considering I moved near the Saw Mill River Parkway, my commuting time to Manhattan, where I worked, had not changed. It took me the same amount of time to get to work as it did when I lived in the Bronx, only this time I no longer had to drive across that dreadful Cross Bronx Expressway. Anyone who has ever driven on it knows what a nightmare it can be no matter what time of day you use it.

After moving to Yonkers, the furthest thing from my mind was to do paranormal investigations or to study the city's history. I just wanted to live in a better neighborhood compared to where I had lived before. However, over the years, I learned of many local hauntings and ghost stories, which got me curious enough to do my own research. In doing so, I became aware of Yonkers' history, and with everything I learned, I became increasingly fascinated.

Yonkers has an incredibly intricate history. Many locations are tied to one another through family ties and geographical location. If there is one thing that fascinates me more than local history, it's the haunted history of a location.

The Yonkers Ghost Investigators is my paranormal team, which was founded in the fall of 2006 with the help of my cousins Christina Claudio and Elijah Levy. Ironically, both are not on the team today. When the team was formed, it consisted of family members and close friends. We only wanted to do it for fun, but I took it seriously from day one. Over the years, some team members lost interest and moved on, while some had to be removed due to other conflicting interests. We've also had new team members added, whom I met through other team members, via the Internet or at my job.

It's interesting that once people know you are into the paranormal, all of a sudden they want to tell you about a ghostly experience they had in their past. It's usually something they rarely spoke about with anyone else, but they know they can tell you because you won't laugh at them or call them crazy. I found this to be the case at work. I heard a lot of stories from the guys at work, which I am sure they didn't tell anyone else.

While the lineup of my team has changed throughout the years, our primary goal remains the same. We aim to seek out evidence of the paranormal, so it can be posted on our website for all to witness.

Together with my team, I have done over three hundred paranormal investigations at numerous locations in Yonkers and in other cities and states, including New Orleans, Gettysburg, Baltimore, Kings Park and Old San Juan in Puerto Rico. During that time, we've gathered enough tangible evidence of the paranormal to show that ghosts truly do exist. Again, our evidence is available on our website.

In this book, I included several locations in Yonkers that are either rumored to be haunted or have been proven to be haunted. I have also included a few random legends I've heard about that I thought were interesting. Rather than be skeptical, check out the evidence and see for yourself. Maybe you will become a believer. At least, maybe you will enjoy the book for its entertainment or historical value.

When I was asked to write this book by The History Press, I was taken aback. I couldn't believe the publisher actually wanted me to write it. At the time, I had never written a real book in my life. I was chosen based solely on the things I wrote on my team's website and also because I mentioned being in the process of writing two books. It was very exciting, since I own a few books published by The History Press.

Initially, it was an incredibly bad time for me. As I stated, I was already working on two other books and didn't really have the time to add a new project. I wasn't retired yet, so I also had my job to consider. It kept me busy most of the week, since I was doing more overtime to prepare for my upcoming retirement.

Regretfully, I asked if I could possibly put this project off for about a year. Much to my surprise, my editor agreed. It was such a relief for me. I dreaded the idea of this project going to someone else. I knew if I was to see this book in its completion written by someone else, I'd regret it for the rest of my life. Luckily, that would not be the case.

By 2014, I now had two books published and I was nearing my retirement date. I felt ready to begin this project, so I informed my contact, Whitney Landis, at The History Press and told her I was ready to begin. She was pleased and gave me the go ahead to start. While I officially began on that day, I had already started preparing notes and had done a lot of research over the previous few months. It gave me a head start, which I needed because I still had to make time to plan for my wedding in May 2014, followed by a month-long honeymoon in Puerto Rico. I did have a few weeks to spare, so I hit the books and wrote out a good portion of this book before May.

Once May arrived, I was married, and within a few days, my wife and I were off to Puerto Rico. During this time, there would be no work done on this project. In fact, I wouldn't get back to it until sometime in mid-July, but even then I didn't accomplish much.

It wasn't until late August that I really got back to working on this book. I went through book after book, learning more about the early history of Yonkers. I spent a lot of money on books, which I thought would be helpful.

They were, but it just meant more reading for me. It's a good thing I like to read and write because I had to do both simultaneously, which saved me a lot of time. For about a year, I had a pile of books on my desk next to my computer. It's nice to see that the entire pile of books has finally been put away on my bookshelves, although I barely have room for them since there are so many.

I was relieved when the book was finally completed, after over a year of reading, researching websites, going to the library or museums, conducting paranormal investigations and going over the evidence. It's a great feeling to know you just wrote a book that will be read by others, including some whom you don't even know.

In this book, I've compiled a list of alleged haunted locations and confirmed haunted locations, which I submit for your scrutiny. I've included evidence gathered during my investigations with my team, as well as documented information from many other witnesses. I tried not to make another history book about Yonkers but instead something a little different.

Most of the photos used either came from my own personal collection, the work of my team members, the Yonkers Historical Society, the Yonkers Public Library, the Library of Congress or from the Internet. None of these photos have been published without the permission of the owner, except in those cases when a photo was listed on the Internet as public domain. In either case I always try to give credit where credit is due, as I would like others to do when using my work.

I do not claim all of these paranormal events mentioned in this book to be fact, since I cannot truly attest to some, unless my team was directly involved. I am merely providing you with these tales so that you can decide for yourself.

All I ask is that you keep an open mind. Don't allow your fears to limit you from what lies beyond your scope of knowledge. There are so many things in this vast universe that remain unknown to us, even after thousands of years of human existence. We are constantly learning and making new discoveries. We cannot expect to see everything with our own eyes in order to believe it exists. Sometimes it's necessary to open your mind to the possibilities around you so you can expand your horizons. Never close your mind to the unknown. There is a wealth of knowledge waiting to be obtained. All we have to do is seek it out, and hopefully through determination, patience and cooperation, we can unlock the mysteries hiding before our very eyes. Dare to think the impossible. It's the only way we can grow into our future.

Imagine if Christopher Columbus had never set sail to prove the world is round. What if Albert Einstein had never developed the Theory of Relativity? What if Orville and Wilbur Wright never made human flight possible?

On that note, thank you kindly for taking the time to read my work. Please, enjoy the book and keep an eye out for my future books.

PART I

RESIDENTIAL HAUNTINGS

IROQUOIS ROAD HAUNTED HOUSE

Long ago, before the United States was a nation, the members of the Native American Iroquois Confederacy made their home in what was known as Mohawk Valley. Located in the north-central region of New York, it was the only true home to the five tribes of this confederation. They never really settled in Westchester County nor had any interest in doing so. However, they often crossed into the land, which at the time was occupied by the Algonquin people. They did so for the purpose of trading, fishing and hunting.

For many years, both groups were at war, until the Iroquois defeated the Algonquin. Regardless of this victory, the Iroquois still did not try to claim the land of their enemy. They were perfectly content where they were.

This allowed the Algonquin to continue to thrive on the lands they called the Aquehung, which included the Tuckahoe Hills and the regions surrounding the Sprain Brook extending to the west banks of the Bronx River. Along the western shore of the Bronx River once stood a great village also called Aquehung, located somewhere around where Tuckahoe and Bronxville currently meet.

The term Aquehung has been interpreted to mean "high bluff," "a river that runs along a high bluff" or simply "a place on the river." It is pronounced *ah-kwa-hung*.

In the time when the Weckquaeskeck, a tribe of the Algonquin, settled in the Aquehung, the residential communities, parkways and railroads that exist today did not surround them. Instead, there was only the unaltered beauty of nature. There were lush forests, dazzling rivers and brooks, rolling hills and pleasant valleys. Wild animals roamed freely and were hunted for food and clothing. The rivers were alive with trout and other freshwater fish. It seemed the Weckquaeskeck had everything they needed in this paradise.

These ancient tribes have forever left their mark in so many ways. By reading books, visiting museums and through Internet searches, we can learn how they lived. Fortunately, some of their legends have survived the ages and are still passed on today.

Throughout Westchester County, there are many streets, towns, rivers and lakes that have retained their original Native American name or are named after a tribe that called New York its home before the land was known as New York.

The Mohegan Heights Section of Yonkers is one such location. Prior to the 1900s, some of the roads that go through the area today did not exist. The area was mostly covered by farmland, which was gradually in development. In time, new roads and homes were built, until one such home was erected on a quiet little corner of a new street called Iroquois Road.

It seems this particular house has a rather interesting past that longs to be told. For one family, a haunting occurred here that was so terrifying that it caused them to move away from New York, never to return.

I came about this account from an anonymous woman who contacted me directly. As a child, she resided within this seemingly normal-looking white house. At a glance, the house gives the appearance of a dream home. It's a two-story brick Colonial-style home built in 1931. A typical white wooden picket fence surrounds the house, which is what you'd expect to find around an average suburban home. Regretfully, without the permission of its current owners, I cannot disclose its exact location or show any images of it, but the address is known to me.

However, on further investigation into its past, the truth is revealed. Within this house, there was once an ominous presence that lurked both down in the eerie basement and up in the attic. "Not a benevolent spirit, but a truly scary and threatening one," my source so nervously stated. I began to wonder what could have possibly happened to her for her to say this to me. I was intrigued and had to know more.

As it turned out, she had no knowledge of the previous owners. It is unknown if anyone ever died within the house.

According to this former resident, she lived there as a child from 1961 to 1978 with her immediate family, which was rather large. She and her seven siblings often felt the unmistakable sensation of heavy breathing on the backs of their necks. Whenever they would turn around, there would be no one there. Sometimes they'd hear the distinctive sound of footsteps walking around the house, but no one could be seen causing the sound. These occurrences happened quite often. She said there were also numerous other family members and friends who have witnessed or experienced these strange incidents, although I was only in contact with the one person.

Throughout the many years the family resided there, they experienced these ongoing occurrences. It took place so many times that for practically the entire time they occupied the house, none of them dared to ascend or descend the basement staircase, unless it was about two steps at a time. They were always in a hurry to get off the staircase for fear that something would happen to them if they lingered too long. Perhaps someone or something might push them or touch them in some way. They also dreaded seeing an apparition appear before their eyes. Fortunately, to the best of her recollection, none of her family members was ever hurt while residing there.

To this day, there is no doubt in her mind that her former home was haunted. She has since moved far away from there and has no intentions to go near the house ever again. Who can really blame her?

Looking south on Iroquois Avenue from Seneca Avenue. Mostly every street in the neighborhood bears a Native American name.

I took a ride to check out the house for myself. It has passed through several owners since my source's family moved out. I was unable to verify from the current owner if any paranormal occurrences take place today. I never went back to try again, not wanting to disturb the current residents, although I did leave them with my card. It is very possible the hauntings came to an end when the other family left. Sometimes it just happens that way. As far as I know, the spirit or spirits did not follow the previous family when they left.

Lee Avenue Hauntings

This residential street goes from north to south and is only several blocks in length. Yet there has been so much paranormal activity that many of its residents felt compelled to move away purely out of fear. Neighbors have often shared and compared their unbelievable stories with one another.

At night, many of them have experienced unseen entities lying down on top of them as they turned in for the night. In the middle of the night, what almost sounded like someone speaking backward has been heard in some homes. The names of neighborhood children were found written in magic marker on the kitchen walls of several homes. Sometimes chairs have been knocked over without anyone being near them.

Donna Parish-Bischoff, a former resident of Lee Avenue, wrote an autobiographical book that describes her horrifying experiences from the time she grew up there. The book is called *The Lee Avenue Haunting*. The following account can be found in her book in more personal detail.

During the early 1900s, long before her family moved into their former home on Lee Avenue, a young British gentleman named Henry Mund lived in this two-story farmhouse on his own. At some point, strange incidents began to take place. He would sometimes write to his mother in Manchester and tell her about how he kept seeing things that he could not explain. Ultimately, these paranormal experiences drove him to madness.

When he no longer resided within the house, it was abandoned and eventually fell into a state of disrepair. It remained that way for nearly two decades.

Finally, someone purchased the property and decided to fix it up. The new owner converted the house into a two-family home. During the time when the house was undergoing extensive renovations, tools would often disappear and turn up at different locations. This usually caused arguments and distrust among the carpenters and contractors. When the house was put up for sale, the families that came to see it would also end up arguing.

It is said there is a dark presence residing within this particular house that has left people with an unsettling feeling. Out of respect for the current owners, I will not disclose the actual address.

The house was finally sold to a family of five. They settled into their new home, totally unaware of the house's supernatural history. Unfortunately, their experiences there did not start out well. The lady of the house hanged herself after only living there for a short time.

According to the suicide note she left for her husband, she no longer wished to be in pain. It is said she suffered from a rare blood disorder and as a result was gravely ill. However, there are those who believe it was the darkness within the house that helped to bring about her fatal decision that would leave her husband and three young children devastated.

It was during the fall of 1974 when the first-floor apartment of the house was leased out to Donna's family. At the time, she was a mere child of six, but she never forgot those early days in that house. She always felt like she was being watched. She said it had been that way before they even moved in.

On the day they went to sign the lease, young Donna had been learning how to play "Mary Had a Little Lamb" on a piano in one of the rooms while the adults conducted their business. The young daughter of the family that was living there at the time was teaching her as a way to keep her entertained.

Suddenly, a lamp fell off the nightstand on its own and broke. The other girl told Donna not to worry because that sort of thing happened often. Like most adults, her father did not believe in ghosts, so naturally Donna was blamed for the mishap. That would only be the beginning for the Parish family.

Donna had an older brother and sister. Together with their parents, they'd reside in the house for many years. During that time, the family went through many dark experiences.

Incidentally, the bulk of Donna's fears came from the basement, which has a separate staircase located at the rear of the house. The washer and dryer were kept down there, and she usually dreaded descending the old steps that led into her own private hell.

Sometimes doors would open or close without anyone touching them. Other times they would slam shut. There would be no wind or breeze to blame. Footsteps could be heard on occasion while there was no one walking.

Disembodied voices were sometimes heard and often sounded like they were speaking another language. There would also be an occasional foul odor that smelled like a filthy animal or urine, which would go just as suddenly as it manifested. On occasion, the family would feel cold spots within the house. It even occurred during the warm summer months. To top it off, whenever holy water was used to bless the house, the amount of paranormal activity would only increase tenfold.

It was the typical otherworldly events you'd expect from any horror movie about a haunted house. The only exception was this was no movie—it was real.

One time, as a child, Donna heard a little girl singing a nursery rhyme from within her bedroom closet. Coincidentally, the song was "Mary Had a Little Lamb." She immediately called for her mother, who came running. When her mother checked the closet, there was no one inside.

Eventually, Donna changed bedrooms and bunked with her sister in a different room down the hall from her original room, which had been next to her brother's room. As it turned out, the room she shared with her sister wasn't much better. There was a lot of poltergeist activity in that room.

Donna recalled asking her sister if she could borrow her shoes to wear around the house. She was still quite young at the time, but her sister gave her permission. She informed Donna the shoes were in their bedroom closet, which was long and narrow. When Donna stepped inside to grab the shoes, she heard a little girl giggle before singing "Mary Had a Little Lamb." Donna instantly let out a scream, and so did her sister, who also heard the disembodied voice.

They soon learned their room previously belonged to the son of the family that resided there before they moved in. Apparently, he ran away before his family moved. He was found dead from a heroin overdose at the Yonkers Motor Inn at around the same time when the paranormal activity in his former room picked up.

Donna's brother once found himself virtually trapped within his bedroom when he opened his door and found all of the dining room chairs neatly piled up like a pyramid against his door. At first, he blamed his sisters, but when he confronted them, they had no idea what he was talking about. They were shocked when they realized the occurrence had been paranormal in nature.

Their mother was literally brought to tears because of the incidents that occurred. One time an unknown thick clear liquid drenched her hair after falling on her head. There were no leaks in the ceiling, so they had no idea where the liquid came from. She rinsed her hair out immediately and cried out of frustration. She even resorted to shouting, "May the powers of Christ compel you," similar to the line used in *The Exorcist* film. It did not work.

Sometimes they would find mysterious puddles of liquid on the floor in random locations throughout their home, but there was never any evidence of a leak. Other times, a yellow syrup-like substance would somehow stain papers left lying about. Donna believes it could have been ectoplasm, a clear liquid-like substance believed to be secreted by spiritual entities when they attempt to manifest into a physical form.

Whenever someone was alone in the house, there was a creepy apparition that would often appear. It was about five feet in height with long dark hair and no visible face. It would start by showing up in someone's peripheral vision, and then it would pop out from somewhere or peek out. Of course, this usually resulted in someone having the living crap scared out of him or her.

That's pretty much what happened when Donna's sister first saw this apparition. She was alone in the kitchen, drawing a picture, when this thing kept peeking from behind her. Finally, when she turned to look, she got the fright of her life and screamed. Her mother came running into the kitchen, but it was gone.

The second time her sister saw this thing was in the bathroom. Once again, she was completely terrified by this creepy vision.

The only one in the household who never admitted to seeing it was their father, who stuck to his guns and refused to believe in ghosts.

Donna also used to see the apparition of a Native American chief. He wore tan clothing with fringes, along with the typical ceremonial headdress and war paint on his face. The feathers in his headdress were bright white, yellow and orange. His eyes were a piercing green color. He almost resembled her father, except his skin was darker and he had long silvery hair. Sometimes he'd be chanting something in his native tongue, while other times he'd open his mouth and no sound would come out.

Whenever Donna saw him, she'd scream. Her mother used to advise her to count to ten and it would go away. Sometime later, her mother revealed to her that she had Mohawk blood running through her veins from her father's side. After she learned about that, she never saw the Native American chief again, but she never forgot how he looked. Could it have been an ancestor visiting her from the other side?

There was another apparition she used to see on occasion. It was a dead boy. Perhaps it was the boy who once lived there. While it is possible, she's never seen what he looked like to compare the two.

A classic Parker Brothers' version of a Ouija board.

Donna once made the mistake of buying an old Ouija board from a flea market at a church. She did so when no one else was near her, spending her last dollar on the musty old game. Her sister was against the idea from the beginning, once she found out. Her mother considered getting a refund, but the man who sold it had already gone.

Back then, Donna did not comprehend the mystical power the Ouija board could contain. She was curious to use her new game—with or without someone else, if need be. She'd sometimes sneak and use it, while no one was watching. Her brother offered to teach her how to use it properly, but by the time he made good on his promise, she had already used it several times on her own.

Had she known then what she knows now about Ouija boards, she would have never bought it. She might have even run from it.

One day, the glass indicator that came with the board flew against the wall and smashed into several pieces. No one was near the board when this occurred. Donna and her brother had just placed it on the dining room table moments earlier, so they could watch television with their mother. In the end, they knew it was for the best.

While playing a magic game with her brother at the age of nine, Donna placed a coat around him from the front, and then he had her tie the sleeves behind his back. With both his hands and feet tied together, he then had her lock him in a closet. Both he and Donna had walkie-talkies, so they could communicate with each other, in case he needed her to help him out. The object of the game was for him to free himself within three minutes, although it didn't turn out that way.

He could not do it, so he called for her to come get him out of the closet. Just as she was about to do so, a male and female could be heard telling her not to do it over the walkie-talkie. They even called her by her name. A chill went down her spine, as she froze in fear. Her brother's muffled screams could be heard from within the closet, and she shrieked in terror, scared for both herself and her brother. Her sister raced down the hallway to free their brother from the closet when she learned he was in there.

When he demanded to know why Donna did not help him, she explained how the voices told her not to do it. She said she became afraid. He was just as afraid and said he felt like someone was in there with him. He even heard breathing next to him.

During one summer, their mother found Donna's name written all over the kitchen pantry in blue cake icing. She thought it was Donna who had written it. When Donna denied it, her mother believed her. They both realized it was probably a ghost who did it. Normally, this would not be an acceptable explanation in most homes. However, this was not most other homes, and there was no one else around when it happened.

To this day, Donna has no idea why her name was written on the pantry.

One early Saturday morning, while she was outside in front of her house listening to her transistor radio, she heard approaching footsteps on the driveway. When she turned to see who it was, she was struck by terror to see a lone pair of long, black, leather boots coming her way. She was so scared she dropped her radio, causing it to break, and ran inside of the house.

Out of all the crazy incidents, there was one that was probably the weirdest that took place. It was night, and Donna was in bed. She watched her sister enter their bedroom, wearing a robe. She walked around the bed behind Donna. When Donna turned to look at her, she was gone. She screamed loudly, causing her mother to run into the room, along with her real sister, who was dressed totally different. She was wearing jeans and a t-shirt.

When a house is haunted by a demonic entity, it's common for that entity to take on the form of another, whether living or deceased. Demons are deceitful liars who sometimes pretend to be innocent children, friends or relatives. They will do anything to gain a person's trust. Once they've gotten close enough, things get particularly dangerous. It can lead to possible demonic possession.

It was bad enough they were already experiencing one of the early stages known as demonic oppression, which is when the demon acts out and makes its presence known by causing malicious mischief.

It didn't take a genius to realize whatever was haunting their home wanted them gone. Unfortunately, due to financial issues, leaving was not an option. They were stuck there, left to deal with whatever else might be coming their way, and they did so for five years.

In 1979, they were asked to vacate the premises by the landlord, who wanted to raise the rent. It was a tough time for them because the move was financially difficult. It would also mean starting school somewhere else, which was usually hard on a kid, let alone three. Yet, in a way, they felt relieved. They would finally be free of the hauntings.

Around three months after moving into their new residence, Donna's brother got the idea to call up their old phone number at the house on Lee Avenue. His eyes practically popped out of his head when he heard a bunch of voices on the other end. It almost sounded like there was a party going on. Men and women could be heard laughing. He passed the receiver around the kitchen, so his mother and sisters could hear the voices. All of a sudden, there was static followed by silence.

They immediately dialed the number, again, but this time they only heard the generic operator recording stating that the number was no longer in service. Her brother was absolutely positive he dialed the correct number both times. There wouldn't be a new family moving into their old residence until another two months later. The question remained. Who did they hear on the other end of the line? Was it the spirits who haunted the house, celebrating their victory over the family?

No one can say for certain. All that can be said is that Donna was fortunate enough to escape from her nightmarish reality with her sanity and life intact. By that time, she had already endured five years of torment and emotional suffering. For most of her childhood, she had to deal with being an insomniac and bouts of depression, which led to overeating. She'd even lost a few friends.

Not many families wanted to associate with people who spoke of seeing ghosts in their home on a regular basis. Back then, people were not as receptive to the paranormal as they might be today.

Currently, Donna resides in Wappingers Falls, New York, which is about an hour north of Yonkers. During her free time, she is a paranormal investigator

It is said numerous homes on Lee Avenue are haunted. This is a view looking north from Sanford Street.

and a co-founding member of IndyPara Paranormal Investigations. Each year before Halloween, she helps organize the village's Halloween Parade, making her a valuable contributing member of her community.

Due to her past experiences, she's become sensitive to the paranormal. She can sense when a spirit is near and can feel when they have unfinished business. In the past, she's also been able to tell when a living person was about to die. The same things that once frightened her as a child now fascinate her. She's learned to embrace these things and has developed a great love for the paranormal.

She feels like she's been given a gift that can be used to help others, whether it is the living or the dead. Her gift is rare and should not be limited to one realm of existence.

She managed to turn her bad experiences into something productive. For that, I have a great deal of respect for her. She's faced her deepest fears and has come out on top. There are many people out there who would sooner turn to drugs or suicide rather than deal with the things she dealt with in that house all those years ago.

That being said, if given the opportunity, I highly recommend buying and reading her book, *The Lee Avenue Haunting*. It's not a long read, and it is worth the minimal amount of time it would take to complete.

As for those of you who currently reside on Lee Avenue and believe your home might be haunted, keep in mind that you are not alone. There are people out there who can help you and are willing to put in the time and effort it takes to do whatever has to be done, but the first step is yours to make. My team is always available, or if you'd like to contact Donna personally, she is also willing to hear from residents of Lee Avenue. Her e-mail address is Vampirella67@yahoo.com.

MONTAGUE PLACE HAUNTED HOUSE

One particular two-story house located on Montague Place is fairly new, built from 2004 to 2005. Prior to its construction, the lot remained vacant for several years. Based on a map from 1899, Montague Place did not even exist yet. There were still many wooded areas around that time, so any structures on the property would have been built during the 1900s.

During the mid-2000s, a family known to me occupied the second-floor apartment of the house, which is located on a hill. While living there, a presence could be felt within the kitchen, usually at night. Shadowy figures were seen moving around by more than one resident. Sometimes the doors would open and close for no reason. The lights would turn on by themselves, especially in the long empty hallway or within the kitchen, which is located at the beginning of the hallway. The television and stereo, which were both in the living room near the entrance of the apartment, have sometimes turned on for no reason with the volume at full blast after they had been turned off with the volume set at a lower level.

One night, the sound of heavy breathing was heard coming from the upper portion of a closet in one of the bedrooms. On another occasion, the same person who heard this breathing said she placed her cellphone on the bathroom sink prior to taking a shower. When she exited the shower, she found her cellphone on the floor. There were no missed messages or calls, so there was no reason the phone would have vibrated and fallen down on its own. Plus, it was placed too far back for it to fall for any other reason. The bathroom door had been locked, so no one else could have knocked it down.

Her father told her how he had to push hard on the front door when entering the house one day because it felt as if someone or something was blocking the door. However, there was no one behind the door. While there

During the night, shadowy figures were seen in this kitchen. The former residents did not spend too much time there alone at night.

was a welcome mat on the floor, it was not high enough to get caught up under the door.

The family has since moved out of the house, and I am unaware if the current occupants have had any experiences. The house has already passed through at least three owners since being built. It's interesting, considering the house is still fairly new. It's not even twenty years old yet. It leaves me to wonder if these families moved out so soon because of something paranormal that might have scared them away.

If anyone reading this happens to reside on Montague Place and you have experienced anything you believe to be paranormal, please feel free to contact my team, Yonkers Ghost Investigators. Our website and my e-mail address can be found toward the end of this book.

I only had one opportunity to do a brief investigation in this apartment. I mainly focused on the kitchen, the bathroom and the bedroom closet. During my time there, I was unable to acquire any evidence at all to back up these claims. However, I do trust the source of these claims implicitly and know her to be truthful and knowledgeable when it comes to the paranormal.

NEPPERHAN AVENUE HAUNTED HOUSE

There is a two-story house located on Nepperhan Avenue that was built in 1957. Decades earlier, the area was occupied by a pickle factory belonging to Wells, Miller and Provost. Sometime after the house was built, the original owner had a concrete deck built at the rear of the backyard to support an Olympic-sized in-ground swimming pool. The house would pass through only two other owners before it became the property of the current owners during the late fall/early winter of 2000. A few years later, a beautiful small fountain was built on the front lawn, which is elevated by a small hill with a built-in rock garden. At a glance, the exterior is not too different from its neighboring houses.

The interior of the house consists of two separate apartments, a walk-in attic, a half-finished basement and a one-car garage. The house is owned by a family that occupies both apartments. However, the members of this family are not the only occupants of the house.

According to the current owners, whispers have been heard mainly in the second-floor bedroom. Voices have also been heard coming from the hallway where the staircase is located. Mysterious footsteps have been heard on the second floor, and people have been touched when no one else is around. The feeling of someone else being on the bed has been felt in both the second-floor bedroom and the first-floor bedroom, which is directly below it. Numerous photos of orbs have been taken in the second-floor living room, although I do not put much stock into photos of orbs.

Those experiences mostly took place during the early 2000s, within the first five years of living there. However, the paranormal activity did not end there.

During a party in the summer of 2008, an elderly female houseguest saw the apparition of a lovely young blond girl of about eighteen years of age. She was walking out of the house from the first-floor kitchen out to the backyard. She then walked up toward the pool area, which is elevated by a concrete deck area. Curious to see who the young blond girl was, the guest walked up to the pool area. By the time she got there, the young girl had vanished. There is nowhere she could have gone from that location, except over the tall fence into a neighbor's yard, which is highly unlikely.

Coincidentally, one resident reported having a strange dream that involved a similar young woman with long, light brown hair named Megan. Before that dream, he had never seen the girl in his life. Could it possibly have been the same girl from the swimming pool, who was now appearing in a dream?

There are people who claim to have been visited by dead relatives or friends in their dreams. As strange as it may sound, it is a common phenomenon.

There have been times when an Ouija board was used within the house on the second floor, mainly in the kitchen. During one Ouija board session conducted in December 2010, which was recorded on video, a bubble-like orb appeared upon request. A strange metallic sound was also heard, as if someone tapped a fork or a spoon.

It is said the use of Ouija boards can lead to spiritual doorways being opened. These doorways can invite unwanted spiritual entities to an otherwise peaceful residence and wreak havoc on a home.

As a warning, it is advised to leave Ouija boards alone. It is not just a game, as some would have you believe, but a communications tool for the paranormal and the occult. In the wrong hands, it could be extremely dangerous. There really is no safe way to use it, and it should *never* be used while alone.

Over the past few years, shadowy figures have been seen moving quickly in front of the second-floor bathroom, which are usually only visible from the corner of your eyes when you are not focusing on them. One resident believes it could be the spirit of her dead black cat, Oscar, mainly because the shadows are often small. The main entrance door of the second-floor apartment leading to the stairs was found open on more than one occasion, during the summer of 2012.

A resident of the first-floor apartment claims she felt as if someone were holding her down while she was waking up from a sound sleep. Of course, it might have been a case of sleep paralysis.

Sleep paralysis is something that usually occurs when a person is either falling asleep or just waking up. The person finds himself or herself temporarily unable to move. It basically feels as if an unseen force is literally holding you down. According to scientific studies, this can be caused by a disruption of REM (rapid eye movement) sleep, which is a time when the body is usually in a dream state. It's a transitional state between wakefulness and rest that is characterized by total weakness in the muscles, or muscle atonia.

Sleep paralysis is often associated with terrifying visions, such as waking to find an intruder in your bedroom. It has also been linked to common disorders such as migraines, narcolepsy, anxiety disorders and obstructive sleep apnea, and it has also occurred while in isolation.

The same first-floor resident spoke of another time a few years earlier when she was lying in her bed and thought her husband was in the room with

Henry Fuseli's *The Nightmare*, created in 1781, depicts a demon holding someone down, thus causing sleep paralysis. *Image provided courtesy of Wikipedia.*

her. She felt him sitting on the bed and noticed when he stood up afterwards. However, at that exact moment, she heard someone else enter the room and it sounded like her husband. She immediately opened her eyes, realizing someone else was in the room with her while she was in bed. She confirmed that it was indeed her husband who had entered the room, but there wasn't anyone else there with them.

She does not like sleeping in her bedroom anymore because she almost always has nightmares there. Her husband also often has nightmares in which he is in mortal danger. Both residents are retired and should rightfully be sleeping more peacefully.

It is unknown if anyone has ever died in their bedroom, but I know the former owner's father died not long before the house was sold.

During several paranormal investigations, the electromagnetic field (EMF) meter has detected a high-energy reading near the wall by the front windows in the living room of the second-floor apartment. EMF meters are scientific devices, which are used to detect energy levels, but it is widely believed they can also detect the presence of spiritual energy. Incidentally, a strong spiritual presence can be felt in more than one room of the second-floor apartment. One has also been felt in an office, which faces the back.

Lately, there is only a minimum amount of paranormal activity that occurs. There have been no negative energies felt within this house.

Old Public School 13

The original Public School 13 building was built in the year 1900. The school originally only had five classrooms, an auditorium and an office for the staff. New additions to the building were added in 1905 and 1910. One of those additions was a new wing that was constructed to the right of the entrance.

The building is located at the corner of McLean Avenue between Park Hill Avenue and Rumsey Road. At the time of its construction, it was considered to be in a rural location and was difficult to reach by any means of transportation available at the time. There were no trolleys or buses that went near it. This was a major concern for the parents of students who attended the school.

According to what I was told in the 1980s, the building's interior was badly damaged in a fire that presumably killed students and teachers. This fire allegedly took place during the mid-1900s, although after months of searching, I have been unable to verify this information and began to doubt its truthfulness.

After this alleged fire, the newer Public School 13 was then built three blocks south on McLean Avenue as an annex to the original building. Classes were eventually moved to the new school building, while the original building underwent repairs.

The original building was later used as an annex for the Board of Education until the 1970s. Unsafe conditions within the building caused the offices to be abandoned. At this point, the original school building was shut down permanently. It remained abandoned for several decades.

I can recall driving past it and seeing it boarded up. I recall hearing the tales about the fire. According to one of my cousins, back when she went to the current Public School 13, there were students who used to sneak into the old boarded-up building after school for thrills.

The original Public School 13 on McLean Avenue during the mid-1900s. It doesn't look too different today. *Courtesy of the Yonkers Historical Society.*

During the early 2000s, the old school building underwent major renovations. It was converted into an apartment building, although according to witnesses, the ghosts of the past still linger on.

A presence can be felt in some apartments, especially on the first floor. Voices have been heard crying out in the dark, and children have been heard laughing or crying. Tenants have seen shadowy apparitions standing near their beds. Could it be the victims of the alleged fire seeking help? The basement laundry room is also said to be haunted.

I knew someone who moved into this building shortly after it was renovated. Valerie lived here with her boyfriend and their young daughter on the first floor facing the front. During that time, she had a few scary experiences, which she told me about. The following experiences occurred in 2006.

While down in the basement laundry room, she heard what sounded like a baby crying. No one else was down there with her at the time. She was certain it wasn't coming from outside or in any of the apartments above. It sounded too close, as if it were in the room with her.

Another time, in her apartment there was a series of snarling noises that were heard by more than one person. Her cousin Kenny was with her at the time, and he also heard these noises.

One time her boyfriend was in bed, and he awoke to see the glowing image of a woman standing in the bedroom. The woman was near his bed. Coincidentally, there was another resident who also had a very similar experience, although I am not sure if it was in the same apartment. It is possible, since Valerie no longer lives in the building.

In 2010, another resident, who also lived on the first floor with his fiancée, had a few experiences of his own. By this time, they had already been living there for three years. He woke up one night and saw what appeared to be a little girl who was probably around five or six years old. She stood in his bedroom facing the wall but then vanished before he could get a good look at her.

This same resident used to hear disembodied voices within the apartment. Sometimes he had dreadful nightmares that would wake him up in a cold sweat.

One particular nightmare left him feeling distraught. A ghostly woman was attacking him, but he was in a different house instead of his own apartment. At some point, they left there and he followed her back to his current residence. Once in his apartment, the woman approached his eleven-month-old son's crib and began to hover over it. His son was asleep in the crib. All of a sudden, the resident woke from his nightmare with a start, only to hear his son screaming and crying in his crib.

The man began to wonder if it had anything to do with his dream. Was there some unseen entity that caused his son to cry or did his son have a similar nightmare? Either scenario is possible.

Like its predecessor, it seems the current Public School 13 building is also haunted. In 1995, there were some students who complained about the bathroom doors swinging open while no one was touching them. A few students reported seeing the ghostly apparition of a little girl wearing a white dress. She would often be seen roaming the halls, although it is unknown if she still roams those halls today.

On April 18, 2007, the original Public School 13 was added to the National Register of Historic Places.

VAN CORTLANDT PARK AVENUE HAUNTINGS

There is a house on Van Cortlandt Park Avenue that is home to at least one spirit. A family that is known to me occupied the two-story house for about one year.

One former resident, Chris, who happens to be one of my Yonkers Ghost Investigators team members, complained that the television would often operate as if someone invisible were in control of it. The channels would change on their own and stop on religious channels. This took place more than once.

His spouse claimed she sometimes felt as if someone were there with her, even when she was at home alone. She said it felt like someone was always watching her. Needless to say, she did not like it one bit. She hated being left home alone at night, which usually meant Chris could not join the team on too many late-night paranormal investigations.

Unfortunately, we only did one investigation at this home. There were too many other people around at the time, which contaminated any possible evidence we might have gotten. As far as I know, we were unable to capture any evidence of the paranormal that could help to back up the claims made.

According to an anonymous female resident of 632 Van Cortlandt Park Avenue, which is located a few blocks to the north of this house, there is a haunted apartment on the sixth floor of that building. Things would sometimes fall down or move on their own, and the toilet would often flush almost nonstop whenever she went out, only stopping after she got home. Her mother, who lived in the same apartment before her, also believed the apartment was haunted.

Supposedly, from what she said, there was a woman who was murdered in the building, although I am uncertain if this took place on the sixth floor. The woman's body parts were chopped up and disposed of piece by piece via the dumbwaiter. Sometime afterward, the dumbwaiters were all sealed off for good to avoid a similar incident from taking place.

I have tried to find any truth to this incident, but so far I cannot verify it. The building was constructed in 1969, so if it happened, it was not that long ago.

Coincidentally, this same apartment building just happens to be where my ex-girlfriend used to reside with her sisters and parents. In fact, her father still lives there today. Her cousins also lived in the building during the time when she still lived with her parents.

Above: Several old houses can be seen in this photo looking south on Van Cortland Park Avenue.

Right: The awning on this block is the entrance to 632 Van Cortlandt Park Avenue.

When I asked her and one of her cousins if they had any knowledge of the building being haunted, neither of them had any recollection of anything ever happening there. However, her cousin did tell me how he "always found it kind of creepy." They also had no knowledge of this alleged murder.

I have personally never experienced anything paranormal within that building, while inside or outside of the building. Of course, I have never gone beyond the third floor with exception of one very brief visit to the rooftop, during the mid-1990s.

WALNUT STREET HAUNTED BOARDING HOUSE

In 1919, there was a three-story apartment building that once stood at 436 Walnut Street in the historic Nodine Hill area of Yonkers. At the time, the building was being used as a boarding house for six different families.

The families constantly complained to the landlord about ghostly activity that kept occurring both in and outside of the building. The occurrences were so frequent it was making their lives a living hell. One of the more common complaints was that someone, or something, enjoyed yanking the bed sheets off of the beds, especially when someone was lying in bed.

A resident from one of the third-floor apartments claimed to have seen an apparition leap from the roof and fall past the window to the ground below. During the fall, a long blood-curdling moan was heard, which caused the resident's blood to run cold. When the resident looked down, there was no one on the ground. Other witnesses claimed they also saw the apparition leap out from the other side of the building. Once again, it let out a long eerie moan.

At first, the landlord did not pay much attention to his tenants, believing them all to be either liars, pranksters or simply out of their minds. Meanwhile, the occupants were all convinced there was at least one ghost haunting their neighborhood. Considering their building was only a few short blocks away from Oakland Cemetery, it wasn't too far-fetched for them to believe.

Finally, he went to the building to check things out for himself. Soon, he began to see and experience strange things he could not explain. He began to realize his tenants might have been telling the truth.

Tired of dealing with the hauntings, his tenants made demands for him to either get rid of the pesky ghost or to call the police so *they* could get rid of it. They threatened to move elsewhere if nothing was done. Under the pressure of his tenants, the landlord gave in. Not knowing what else to do, he contacted the Yonkers Police Department and insisted they send someone to conduct an investigation.

Two detectives were dispatched to the residence. They began their investigation by interviewing each of the tenants. It didn't take too long to notice how deeply disturbed the tenants were by the haunting. If this were a joke, it was a good one because every tenant appeared to be sincere with his or her statements.

One particular tenant gave her story, claiming to have seen the apparition with her own eyes. She said at first she used to hear odd noises in the hallway, down in the basement, up on the rooftop and even within the walls. She tried to locate the source of these noises, believing she'd find rodents.

However, the moment she saw a white flash fall past her window from the roof to the ground, she gave up her search. Whatever had fallen made no sound as it fell. She ran to the window and looked down to the ground, but there was no one and nothing unusual down below. She was baffled.

She recalled an incident from the past, in which a woman and her child had burned to death. It happened many years earlier. I am uncertain if it took place in the same building or in a building that existed prior to this one. She figured it was their spirits she had seen and heard trying to escape the flames.

There was another tenant, who had never seen any ghosts, although he did hear moaning and what sounded like a ghost moving about the house on more than one occasion.

One gentleman was so frightened that he left his apartment behind and settled for sleeping elsewhere. He made this decision after one fateful night. He had just fallen asleep in his bed shortly after midnight. He left his window open for ventilation.

All of a sudden, he felt his bedsheets get yanked off the bed. When he awoke, he saw something white enter through the window. It floated up toward the ceiling and disappeared out of sight.

Oddly, the detectives were ordered to remain at the boarding house and wait for the ghost to reappear. This is something that would definitely not happen today. Apparently, it must have been a slow night, with regard to crime.

The detectives waited out the ghosts by hiding on the first-floor hallway of the building. Shortly after midnight, they heard what sounded like moans accompanied by other strange noises. It sounded like it was coming from above them on the second floor. They ran upstairs but were unable to identify a source for these sounds. There was no one else in the hallway.

Looking south on Walnut Avenue where the boarding house used to stand at the far end of the park, which didn't exist at the time.

At this point, they agreed to wait outside instead. They went outside and across the street, where they stood watching the building from a safe distance. That's where they waited for the rest of the night.

By morning, they left and returned to their station house. Their mission had been unsuccessful. Instead, they both felt utterly confused and obviously startled by their experience.

This old Walnut Street apartment building is no longer standing. It was torn down to make space for new development and has been gone for quite some time. Trinity Plaza Park and a few newer homes are now on its former site.

PART II

NON-RESIDENTIAL LOCATIONS

ALDER MANOR AND THE BOYCE THOMPSON INSTITUTE

Alder Manor is located on North Broadway in the northwest region of Yonkers, between Executive Boulevard and Odell Avenue, just south of the Lenoir Nature Preserve. The Croton Aqueduct Trail runs through the woods on a steep slope at the far western side of the estate.

Built high on a hill that once boasted one of the finer views of the Palisades, this Italian Renaissance Revival mansion was designed by the architectural firm of Carriere and Hastings of New York City for diamond mining millionaire William Boyce Thompson. He began purchasing land in the northwestern region of Yonkers in 1906 and continued buying up land through 1910, when he acquired the land he would call the Alders. Alder Manor would be built there by 1912. The inspiration for its construction came from his hometown of Alder Gulch in Virginia City, Montana. Thompson originally intended the manor to be a weekend residence, while he worked on Wall Street in Manhattan.

Surrounding Alder Manor were fabulous gardens that once rivaled those of the nearby Untermyer Park with its columns, gazebo, fountains and fine statues. The gardens were created with the intention of imitating those of classic Greece and Italy. It included beautifully designed relics from those locations, although today the gardens are a mere memory of what they once were. Ironically, it more resembles the ruins of ancient Greece and Italy today.

Soon after moving to Yonkers, Thompson became involved in politics, but his interests would soon expand. He was already a mining tycoon, a politician and a leading financial advisor to many of New York's wealthiest citizens during the early part of the twentieth century. Next, he would become a plant researcher.

In 1917, after Thompson took a trip to Russia, the level of poverty and starvation he encountered there left him feeling extremely troubled. He began looking at agriculture as being of the utmost importance for a nation in order for it to maintain its population growth. He was soon inspired to do something about it.

On September 24, 1924, he established the Boyce Thompson Institute for Plant Research, on the other side of North Broadway behind where the Applebee's now stands. The institute was a way for him to learn more about plants and how their natural development could be stimulated by the regulation of elements that normally contribute to their existence. Thompson named his institute in honor of his parents, Anne Boyce and William Thompson. He endowed it with $10 million of his own money and was able to receive government support for his project. In time, revenues from the licensing of the institute's patents also helped to fund the institute. At one time, the institute consisted of more than three hundred acres of rich agricultural land with a multitude of greenhouses built for botanical research.

When Thompson died in 1930, he left his trust and estate to his wife and daughter, under the condition they continue to reside at Alder Manor. His family resided there until the mid-1900s.

The Boyce Thompson Institute, circa September 1924. *Courtesy of the Yonkers Historical Society.*

Alder Manor when it was Mary Elizabeth Seton High School. *Courtesy of the Yonkers Historical Society.*

When his daughter, Gertrude Thompson, last of the family owners, passed away in 1950, Alder Manor was willed to the Roman Catholic Archdiocese of New York. It became the Mary Elizabeth Seton High School, making it the first Catholic school in the city of Yonkers. It served as a high school for ten years before being upgraded to a junior college in 1960.

During this time, there were a few modifications made, including the construction of a chapel and the addition of a fire escape and dormitory building. There were also many modifications made within the manor to transform rooms into bedrooms, classrooms and offices.

Former student John Tantillo fondly recalls his time as a student at the school. During his free time, he would often go exploring with his friends. Once they were surprised to find a few graves next to the garden of the old mansion. There are also some in the next-door Lenoir Nature Preserve. The students were not allowed in that area, but that didn't stop them from sneaking a peek every once in a while.

On another occasion, John saw a locked door that led down to an off-limits underground area beneath the manor. The students heard many rumors about an underground tunnel system that went all the way to

Untermyer Park, but the only tunnel John ever went into was that of the old Croton Aqueduct Trail, which he coincidentally accessed from an old pump house at Untermyer Park. It is very likely this was the tunnel he originally heard about.

John and his friends used to spend a lot of their free time hanging out around the school grounds and in the nearby park. He was told how satanic cultists used to do rituals in the area at night, but he didn't believe it, until he saw something one day that changed his mind: a group of people dressed in long, dark hooded robes lurking around the Croton Aqueduct Trail near the Lenoir Nature Preserve.

Similar stories about satanic cult activity were told when it came to Untermyer Park during the same era. Convicted serial killer David Berkowitz (aka the Son of Sam) also confirmed these stories. For more details on that, refer to the section in this book on Untermyer Park.

Mary Elizabeth Seton Junior College closed in 1989, after merging with Iona College. Eventually, Alder Manor was neglected and abandoned for several years. Thieves and vandals would usually break in to loot items, get drunk or get high. During the mid-1990s, an old stained-glass window was stolen from the front of the former chapel.

In time, rumors went around claiming that the mansion was haunted. This was supposedly one of the main reasons why the sisters of the college

The creepy-looking old chapel located at the rear of the manor can be seen in this photo taken in March 2012.

originally felt the need to abandon these once extravagant grounds. It was alleged that unexplained mischief, which appeared to be paranormal in nature, would often occur at the school.

Some of the ghosts said to haunt the manor are celebrities who once partied there in its heyday. The list includes Josephine Baker, Big Mamma Cass, Andy Warhol and John Belushi.

Whether there is any truth to this is beyond my knowledge. I've never seen or heard any evidence to back this up. While I did learn of it being haunted soon after becoming a paranormal investigator, I never got the chance to check it out with my team. Our calls made to the location were not returned, and there are security cameras watching the grounds around the manor, so sneaking in is not advised.

Sometime around 2004, an Irish-American cultural organization named Tara Circle acquired the manor. The group used it as a cultural center and often rented it out for special events in order to raise money for ongoing renovations. I heard the group no longer owns the property, so I am unsure of the current owners. The Foxfire School, a public school, is located on the grounds just south of the old manor.

The manor was placed on the National Register of Historic Places in October 1982. It has become one of the city's most favored locations, enticing photographers and filmmakers from all around. It has served as the filming location for popular films such as *Mona Lisa Smile* and *A Beautiful Mind*.

In 2014, there were rumors going around that there are underground tunnels linking Alder Manor to the Boyce Thompson Institute, which was abandoned in 1978, subsequent to becoming part of Cornell University. Considering that my team and I had already conducted a paranormal investigation at the Boyce Thompson Institute and explored it fully, I had my doubts about these rumors, so I set out to find proof.

We returned to search for these alleged tunnels. First, we checked around the old greenhouses. There are staircases that lead under the greenhouses down into one large basement, which connects each greenhouse to the main building of the institute. A huge connecting basement does not constitute an underground tunnel system to me.

We did find an opening in the greenhouse area that leads down to a small L-shaped maintenance tunnel, although it doesn't go very far. It goes from beneath the greenhouse to under the old workshop, but there is no access to the workshop. The only entry points are from the basement of the greenhouses and from an access hatch in the upper greenhouse area that is only a few feet away from the entrance to the workshop. There is

The greenhouses today are mostly devoid of glass.

This photo was taken within the maintenance tunnel, after turning east. It soon comes to an end. There is a dead end to the north.

also a sealed door that used to lead from the outside to the maintenance tunnel. This tunnel does not connect to Alder Manor, nor are there any other tunnels under the Boyce Thompson Institute, as far as we can tell.

COPCUTT MANSION

John B. Copcutt arrived from England during the 1840s. He settled at Yonkers, where he built a veneer sawmill along the Saw Mill River southwest from Philipse Manor Hall. Between 1853 and 1854, he built his Italian-style villa, the Copcutt Mansion, on Nepperhan Avenue. Copcutt resided in this two-and-a-half-story mansion with his wife and eventually with their children.

Soon after its construction, rumors began to circulate about the mansion being haunted. During the late 1860s, people used to gather around the old mansion hoping to catch a glimpse of ghostly apparitions. The occurrences became so popular that the *Yonkers Herald* newspaper printed headlines about the supposedly haunted mansion of Nepperhan Avenue. For a long time, it was the city's only ghost story.

It is not known what Copcutt's opinion was on the matter. In 1895, he died at the age of ninety and was buried at the Saint John's Cemetery in Yonkers. His widow continued to live in the mansion until her death four years later. Within a year, the mansion was sold to Saint Casimir's Roman Catholic Church.

In 1900, the sisters of the parish were the first to move in. They used it as a convent for a while, but none of them ever saw anything to give them reason to believe the convent was haunted. Some of them were actually disappointed about not seeing any ghosts but not surprised. They believed the late Monsignor Dworzak, who was the founder of Saint Casimir's Roman Catholic Church in Yonkers, had driven out whatever was haunting the mansion at the time of the purchase. He went through the entire mansion with holy water like a man on a crusade.

At some point, the entire structure was moved from its original location to its current location, and the church was built in its place.

In 1957, the former Copcutt Mansion was converted into the rectory of Saint Casimir's Roman Catholic Church. According to a former pastor, Monsignor Vincent Raith (ideal last name), he had never seen anything out of the ordinary while residing there. As of July 1972, the pastor, Reverend Edmund A. Fabisinski, and his assistant pastors, Reverends Joseph R.

The former Copcutt Mansion as it appears today.

Kozlowski and Eugene Kosnik, had also never witnessed anything strange at the rectory.

Lilian Leale was one of Copcutt's last surviving grandchildren. She was the daughter of Rebecca Copcutt and Dr. Charles Leale, the very same doctor who worked on President Abraham Lincoln at the time of his assassination. The couple actually got married in the mansion.

According to an interview with Miss Leale by the *Yonkers Herald*, she had only fond memories of being in the mansion as a child. She could easily remember the huge Christmas trees that decorated the main hall each December. During the summer she'd enjoy seeing the wonderful English gardens outside the house. She never once saw a ghost on the property.

A Hastings-on-Hudson resident named Frank Mack was a tenant in the house while working as an assistant vice-president of the old First National Bank in Yonkers. He said he could recall that the trolleys that went by on Nepperhan Avenue would cast eerie shadows on the windows of the attic. Anyone looking at the windows from the outside might think ghostly shadows were moving about within the house.

The rectory is located at 239 Nepperhan Avenue, near where the avenue merges with Yonkers Avenue. On September 12, 1985, it was added to the National Register of Historic Places.

GLENWOOD POWER PLANT, AKA THE GATES OF HELL

The Glenwood Power Plant, located at 2 Glenwood Avenue, served as the generator for the New York Central Railroad and later for the Consolidated Edison Company of New York. It was built between 1904 and 1906 for the purpose of storing electrical generators, which powered the nearby railroad. It included an adjacent switch house and a substation that was housed in a separate building.

The boiler room was located in the southern half of the main building. It accommodated twenty-four boilers, which were kept beneath two 3,500-ton-capacity coalbunkers. Coal deliveries were done via train or barge, since the power plant borders the Hudson River on one side.

The northern half of the building housed the turbine room, where four powerful 5,000-kilowatt Curtis turbo-generators were placed. Each one stood at an incredible thirty-five feet in height. While there was room for six turbo-generators, only four were ever installed. The initial output they gave off was 20,000 kilowatts. It was more than enough to supply power for the entire electrified zone of both the Hudson and Harlem lines.

On the outside of this industrial powerhouse were twin brick smokestacks that shot straight up into the sky towering over the structure. They could be seen from miles away, making the power plant easily one of the most recognizable landmarks along the lower Hudson River Valley.

When the power plant was built, there was special attention given to the design of the windows. The designers wanted the building to fit in with its environment, while allowing a maximum amount of natural light to enter the interior during the daytime. Therefore, large arched windows were installed all around the lower half of the main building. At night, the light from within the power plant would give off a dazzling appearance for those that lived nearby.

The power plant operated under the ownership of the New York Central Railroad until 1936. At that point, it was sold to the Yonkers Electric Light and Power Company, which was a subsidiary of the Consolidated Edison Company of New York. By then, it had become much cheaper and easier for the railroad to buy power, rather than to supply it with large costly power plants.

By 1950, the power plant was one of the three main sources of power for the rapidly developing city of Yonkers. However, there were plans in motion to build a better, more efficient powerhouse using improved modern technology. Thus, the old power plant was put on standby until it was permanently closed down in 1963.

A ferry approaching Yonkers Pier from the south, before the power plant was completed, circa 1905–6. *Library of Congress.*

Over the next few decades, the Glenwood Power Plant began to decay due to neglect and abandonment. Its once powerful boilers and turbines were sold for scrap metal. The windows now had missing or broken glass. Graffiti covered the walls both on the inside and outside. The floors within were strewn with broken glass, pieces of rotted wood, shards of rusted metal and garbage.

I recall my first view of the power plant during the early 1990s. Rumors were going around that it was haunted. Strange noises could sometimes be heard coming from within. On a rare occasion, you could even hear someone scream. The power plant had its fair share of trespassers. People would often sneak inside to get drunk or high. Gangs turned it into their playground. Urban explorers were eager to sneak into the building for a photo session within one of Yonkers' most popular landmarks.

I must admit I was tempted to explore it to conduct a paranormal investigation. The only reason I never did was because I did not wish to

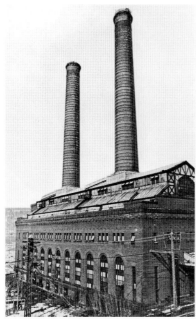

Glenwood Power Plant after its completion in the early 1900s, compared with a photo when it was abandoned. *Courtesy of the Yonkers Historical Society.*

endanger anyone who would have gone with me. I certainly had no intention of going in alone.

It was a good thing I never did go inside. In 2008, Jim Bostic of the Yonkers Gang Prevention Coalition and councilwoman Patricia McDow reported that gangs held brutal initiations within the power plant that sometimes involved up to three hundred individuals, severe beatings and deviant sexual behavior. It was this revelation that would earn the power plant its reputation as the Gates of Hell.

The Glenwood Power Plant has been referred to as one of the most remarkable ruins along the Hudson River. The twin smokestacks stand out from a distance and are a constant reminder of Yonkers' early industrial history. Nearly every Yonkers resident recognizes it immediately. In a way, it does what the Empire State Building does for New York City. It supplies a highly recognizable landmark that can be associated with the city. Of course, it may not be as visually stimulating, but it belongs to Yonkers and we are proud to have it.

In 2008, the Preservation League of New York State named it as one of the seven most endangered sites in the state. After being abandoned for

This page: The interior of the Glenwood Power Plant as it appeared during the early 2000s. *Courtesy of Rob Yasinsac (www.hudsonvalleyruins.org).*

decades, it was purchased by a private developer who took steps to convert it into a convention center.

In 2013, renovations began, which included clearing out old machinery and equipment, broken glass and other debris. When completed, the iconic power plant will ultimately be converted into an expo center called the Power House. Plans are to build it up into an event complex focused on the arts, with a restaurant, a luxury hotel and a marina. Phase one of the conversion is not expected to be complete until around 2016 with an estimated cost of $70 million. Phase two will include the restaurant, hotel and the addition of an improved marina. It is expected to take around ten years to complete at a cost of about $80 million.

The John F. Kennedy Marina is currently located nearby. It is not much now, but it is a place where boats can be launched into the Hudson River.

The Glenwood Metro-North Railroad station situated right next to the old power plant still serves the residents of the Glenwood neighborhood of Yonkers via the Hudson Line. On weekdays, trains leave every half hour bound for New York City's Grand Central Terminal, which is about a forty-minute ride away.

HUDSON RIVER GHOSTS AND LEGENDS

The discovery of the Hudson River is officially credited to famous English explorer Henry Hudson. At the time, Hudson had been working on behalf of the Dutch East India Company. Originally, he set sail from Amsterdam in search of a northwest passage to China but instead found himself at the southern tip of what would someday become New York City.

On September 13, 1609, Hudson sailed his ship, *De Halve Maen*, which translates to the *Half Moon*, up the river that now bares his name. The ship wasn't very big. It measured only eighty-five feet in length. The men were in cramped quarters and disliked their captain. They were on the verge of mutiny before finally arriving at North America. In time, this discovery would lead to the colonization of New York first by the Dutch and then by the British.

One legend associated with the river not many people are aware of is that of the Hudson River monster nicknamed "Kipsy." Much like the Loch Ness monster of Scotland, Champ of Lake Champlain or Caddy of Canada, this legend is based on myriad unconfirmed sightings and rumors. There is

An artist's rendering of *De Halve Maen* (*Half Moon*). *Courtesy of the Yonkers Historical Society.*

virtually no tangible evidence to support the stories that go along with these legendary cryptids, aside from some questionable photos and videos.

A cryptid is basically a beast of legend whose existence has yet to be proven scientifically. Sometimes photos are submitted, but they can usually be explained away as hoaxes or misidentifications.

The myth of sea monsters goes way back to the earliest days of sea exploration, when it was believed the world ended at some point and ships would fall off into oblivion if they dared sail beyond the edge. The earliest sea explorers began these tales at the first sight of large underwater creatures they had never seen before, such as whales, giant squids, jellyfish, manta rays, walruses, manatees and certain species of large fish, such as sturgeon, which can grow up to eight feet in the Hudson River.

The Algonquin Native Americans believed there was a giant deadly sea monster called the *Mishibijiw*, which was basically a type of water panther that lived in deep waters. It was a cross between a cougar and a sea dragon. This creature was sometimes described as being furry, with antlers or horns, a long prehensile tail that looked as if it were made from copper and what looked like sharpened teeth going down its back. The *Mishibijiw* was often blamed for the drowning of Native American men and women.

According to other Algonquin legends, there were also small water spirits called *Memegwesi* that dwelled along the riverbanks. These child-sized spirits were described as hairy with large heads and strange voices that sounded like the whine of a dragonfly. It's believed they originated from the bark of trees. They were usually blamed for causing canoes to go off course or for random thefts. Sometimes they would even carve symbols on the rocks along the river.

The Book of the Great Sea-Dragons by Thomas Hawkins shows a plesiosaurus and temnodontosaurus in battle at the so-called world's edge. *Courtesy of Wikipedia.*

I wonder if these so-called spirits were actually manatees. To a person who has never seen a manatee, it would probably inspire several strange ideas at the sight of one basking in the river, surfacing for air briefly. They are often referred to as sea cows due to their large size.

Manatees can grow up to thirteen feet long and weigh as much as 1,300 pounds. They use paddle-like flippers to help them swim. They tend to inhabit warm, shallow coastal areas and rivers but have been known to frequent the Hudson River.

Other types of fish found in the Hudson are American eel, American shad, Atlantic sturgeon, channel catfish, northern pike, northern pipefish and striped bass. All can grow to rather large sizes.

The Hudson River monster sightings began in the 1600s. The Algonquin told of a legendary sea serpent that resided in the river's waters. The sightings were usually of a hump or humps seen moving through the water, which is similar to most sightings at Loch Ness. The waves sometimes move in a way that it looks as if something large is swimming by when in fact there is nothing there. However, sometimes there was also unexplained splashing seen in the river. Of course, there are many sea creatures that splash.

Henry Hudson's crew aboard the *Half Moon* spotted what they believed to be a sea monster in 1610, while sailing along the river.

In March 1647, Adriaen Cornelissen van der Donck, the patroon of the area that would someday become Yonkers, spotted several whales swimming up the river going as far as Troy. One of these whales perished at the Cohoes Falls, causing the river to become oily for the next three weeks. While this was not a sea monster sighting, it is documentation that a whale could find its way into the river and possibly be mistaken for something else.

There was another supposed sea monster sighting farther north, near Clermont at the Livingston estate in 1807.

In June 1899, a group of young men were bathing in the river near Weehawken, New Jersey, when they were chased out of the water by something large. The first witness saw it heading toward him, and after letting out a scream, he immediately made haste for the shore. The unknown underwater creature then went after the next swimmer, who also raced to the shore unscathed. By this time, all the swimmers hurried to get out of the water. At this point, the creature splashed the water loudly with its tail and swam away.

Some witnesses described it as a shark, while others claimed it was a sea serpent. It was said to be between twelve to eighteen feet in length. This sighting was published in the *New York Times*.

While it took place in New Jersey, I felt it was necessary to mention since there are no walls underwater stopping the creature from coming toward New York and farther up into Yonkers. If it were indeed a shark, no one would expect to see it near the shores of Yonkers, where it could be mistaken for something it is not.

The crew of the *Clearwater* steamboat spotted something moving along the river in the early 1900s.

In the summer of 2006, people began to believe the Hudson River Monster had returned after there were multiple sightings of something unusual moving north and south along the river between Manhattan and Poughkeepsie. It turned out to be a large manatee, which generally stick to warmer waters hundreds of miles to the south. However, on occasion they have been spotted as far north as Rhode Island, but it is usually during warm summer months when the water temperature heats up.

The rumors of a manatee in the river started up again two years later when there were more sightings, which confirmed these rumors.

I doubt there is a sea monster living in the Hudson River. Most of these sightings can be explained as sharks, manatees or some other practical sea creature. At the same time, I do believe it could be possible for some sort of undiscovered sea creature or relic from the past to be the cause of many other sightings around the world. It's quite easy for a plesiosaur to hide in the depths of the sea and remain unseen. There are still so many new underwater species being discovered every year, so it is possible.

It should be no surprise that the river is said to be haunted, considering the amount of ghost stories that are tied to the Hudson River Valley. In *Knickerbocker's History of New York* by Washington Irving, he mentions that the river is home to many goblins and ghosts.

Sometimes, on dark stormy nights, you may think you are seeing an old wooden sailing ship near the waters of the Tappan Zee Bridge. It just might be possible. Henry Hudson's schooner the *Half Moon* is said to haunt these waters and mainly appears at night during harsh weather.

In addition, the ghost ship, or "storm ship," as it has been called, has been frequently spotted near Pollepel (Pollopol) Island, home to the eerie Bannerman Castle. The island is supposedly haunted. Rumor has it that Henry Hudson and his crew witnessed ghostly figures on the island during their exploration of the river. The Native Americans in the region avoided the island out of fear.

According to legend, the notorious pirate Captain Kidd could have left buried treasure at any point along the entire Hudson River Valley, including in Yonkers. Not to mention, there are allegedly many other possible locations along the Atlantic Coast. There are even legends about people seeing the ghost of his sunken ship beneath the water with its masts still standing tall.

The Hudson River was also the site of one of the worse steamboat disasters in New York's history. On the morning of July 28, 1852, the *Henry Clay* set out from the river port at Albany and made its way south on the Hudson River. It was a warm, sunny day, with temperatures rising to the eighties by the peak of the day. As the boat went past Yonkers just before 3:00 p.m., a fire broke out. It raced up from the engine room and quickly spread to the midsection. A panic immediately ensued as people began shouting to warn the others about the fire.

The ship's captain immediately maneuvered the boat toward the eastern shore and New York, as there was only the Palisades on the New Jersey side. It was at least one mile from the nearest shore, which was a beach at Riverdale near the Hudson River Railroad tracks. The boat crashed bow first at full speed onto the shore and ran aground about thirty feet on the shore.

At the time, there were an estimated five hundred passengers onboard. Many ran aft toward the stern, the rear of the boat, to get as far from the impact as possible. This would prove to be a fatal mistake because the fire trapped them, leaving only one way to reach the shore. They'd have to jump down into the river, which was fairly deep in that area. Many did not know how to swim and had to decide between burning to death and drowning.

Only twenty-three bodies were recovered on the day of the disaster. By the next day, there were a lot of people who were missing. It took several days to locate some of the missing bodies, and most had to be identified by the clothing they wore. Nearly eighty people perished as a result of the wreck. Some victims came from prestigious families, which made the incident more newsworthy than it probably would have been. The disaster became known as "the Hudson's blackest day."

Considering the amount of deaths from that day, it wouldn't surprise me if the shore where the boat crashed was haunted by some of these unfortunate souls.

Another story I came across was told by a Yonkers resident who preferred to remain anonymous. It's unknown if this witness is female or male, and I'm not sure when or exactly where this sighting took place.

Supposedly, this person has seen the ghost of a Native American woman on more than one occasion near the river in an undisclosed location of Yonkers. The ghost was seen wandering around desperately, as if she were

Burning of the Henry Clay *Near Yonkers* by Nathaniel Currier. *Courtesy of the Yonkers Historical Society.*

in search of something or someone. Perhaps she is searching for a lost child or lover who drowned.

The anonymous witness claims to have seen the apparition on two separate occasions. During the first sighting, the person was alone. There were no other witnesses. However, for the second encounter, the person was with his or her young daughter, who also saw the ghost. This immediately became apparent when the daughter specifically pointed out the Native American woman. Unfortunately, it was at that moment that the woman mysteriously vanished into thin air. There was no mention of whether the ghost made a sound or acknowledged their presence.

There are a few possible locations where the sightings might have occurred. One place is the esplanade near the downtown area of Yonkers. It could also have been near the boat launch, close to the Glenwood Power Plant. Considering Yonkers borders the river, there are numerous possibilities.

I have been unable to find any other similar stories to back this one up, but that does not make it false. When there are at least two witnesses, I feel more inclined to believe a sighting could have taken place. Children tend to be reliable witnesses, as they have no real need to create hoax stories, except maybe to get out of trouble or to impress their friends. This was clearly not one of those situations.

It is a well-known historic fact that Native American Algonquin people once inhabited the area. There were at least two tribes that lived in Yonkers:

the Weckquaeskeck, who came from the north, and the Manhattan from the south. If there is a Native American spirit haunting the riverbanks of the Hudson, she probably belonged to one of those tribes.

Could it be this poor Native American woman still doesn't realize she has passed on to the spirit world? Maybe she has unfinished business to complete before she can move on. It would be nice to know exactly what or whom she is searching for, since it has kept her spirit roaming these lands. Perhaps her death was the result of a tragic love story. Someone could have murdered her, and now she may be seeking her body because it was carelessly dumped in the river or secretly buried along the riverside. It's also possible she might have died at the hands of Dutch settlers.

During the Indian Wars of the early 1650s, Dutch settlers butchered many Native Americans needlessly. Some natives were thrown into the river and forced to drown. It could be this poor Native American woman met her end in this way, or perhaps her child or another loved one was thrown into the river. Perhaps now she spends eternity searching for that person in a hopeless attempt to rescue them.

Unfortunately, we will most likely never know the true answer. All the same, I will continue searching, and hopefully, if I get lucky, I can make contact with her spirit someday or learn her story. It would be nice to help her move on and finally find peace in the afterlife, which her people strongly believed in.

OAKLAND AND SAINT JOHN'S CEMETERIES

Oakland Cemetery is located on Saw Mill River Road and Ashburton Avenue. Right next door to it, on the same grounds, is Saint John's Cemetery, the oldest cemetery in Yonkers. From a distance, both appear to be one cemetery, but they are in fact two separate locations.

In 1751, Frederick Philipse gave this land to the Saint John's Parish. A rectory was built in 1770 near where the entrance to the Saint John's Burial Ground would be about a decade later. In 1778, during the American Revolutionary War, a battle was fought in the area. Soon, the need for more burial grounds became evident.

By 1783, the Saint John's First Public Burial Ground was established just north of the rectory. It belonged to the Saint John's Parish. The first burial was Richard Archer, who resided at the rectory. In fact, the cemetery was built in around his grave, as it did not exist until after his death. The knoll on the northwest part of the glebe was where he wished to be buried. Some soldiers who died during the Revolutionary War were among the first to be interred at the new cemetery. Soon, many local families buried their dead here as well. Among them are members of the Fowler, Getty, Odell, Shonnard, Waring and Weed families.

Many of the oldest graves in Yonkers can be found at Saint John's Cemetery, which is a rectangular area situated on a hill bordering the northwest corner of Oakland Cemetery. There are still gravestones that can be read clearly that date back to the 1700s. The rectory was demolished in 1845, clearing the way for more grave sites.

In 1852, when the steamboat *Henry Clay* caught fire in the Hudson River and lost nearly eighty of its passengers to fire or drowning, ten of the victims were buried at Saint John's Cemetery. At the time, eight of them had not been identified.

There were two separate funeral services held for the unidentified victims. The first took place on Friday, July 30, 1852, and included a service at the Reformed Dutch Church. As the cart carrying the coffins slowly made its way to the cemetery, thunder crashed overhead and the church bell tolled in the growing distance. It only added to the ominous feeling for those in attendance. The second funeral followed two days later with less dramatic flare. The unidentified victims were laid to rest in donated burial plots numbered from 238 to 248 situated at a high point of the old burial ground overlooking Saw Mill River Road.

In the days following the funeral services, family members seeking their missing relatives were able to identify some of the previously unidentified victims by matching descriptions of the buried with their missing family members. Sadly, three of the interred victims would forever remain without identities.

Sometime later, a marble memorial column was erected marking the site of the victims' last resting place. A local organization called the Odd Fellows was credited with donating the monument. There used to be an inscription that mentioned the names of the victims, but it has since faded away.

About a decade later, local soldiers who fell in battle during the American Civil War were interred here. It was around this time that Yonkers decided to set up additional burial grounds nearby.

Soon after the war, on December 6, 1866, Oakland Cemetery was established for the local residents of Yonkers. It was originally known as the Yonkers Cemetery Association. Its iron gateway entrance at Ashburton

This memorial was erected in memory of the victims of the *Henry Clay* disaster in 1852.

Avenue was added a year later. In 1875, Saint John's Cemetery was incorporated. Years later, in 1905, the iron gateway at Oakland Cemetery was renovated to its current appearance, more or less.

There are a few high-profile Yonkers residents buried at Oakland Cemetery. One of the most famous is Dr. Charles Augustus Leale, the young surgeon who worked on President Abraham Lincoln after he was shot by actor John Wilkes Booth at Ford's Theatre in Washington, D.C., during a performance of *Our American Cousin*. Dr. Leale's grave is located in Section 2 of the cemetery at Nepperhan Avenue bordering the south side of Saint John's Cemetery. He is buried with his wife, Rebecca, daughter of John Copcutt, who is entombed in the crypt directly behind them.

Alexander Smith, founder of the Alexander Smith Carpet Mills, is also buried here on a hill across from his daughter, Eva Smith Cochran, and her husband, William Francis Cochran. The Cochran family is just below the Hilltop Garden in Section 10. Both the Smith and Cochran family plots have obelisks within enclosed circular burial plots. Other family members are interred in the surrounding graves.

Elisha Graves Otis, founder of the Otis Elevator Company, and a few of his family members are interred on the hill directly behind Alexander Smith in a large unmarked family crypt. A small statuette of a doll sits on the steps

Looking toward Oakland Cemetery from the banks of the Saw Mill River, circa the early 1900s. *Courtesy of the Yonkers Historical Society.*

This is the grave of Dr. Charles A. Leale and his wife, Rebecca, with the crypt of her father, John Copcutt, in the background.

of the crypt to indicate where the remains of Elisha Otis were laid to rest. Prior to starting his elevator company, he worked as a doll maker.

In 1927, the County of Westchester purchased fourteen acres of land on the east side of the cemetery for the construction of the Saw Mill River Parkway. The graves in that area were relocated.

Sometime afterward, a few people reported seeing the wandering apparition of a woman at the far eastern edge of the cemetery. No one knows who she was. It is possible she is searching for her lost grave site. As far as I know, there have been no recent sightings of her.

Oakland Cemetery is geographically divided into two halves by a hill, which separates the western lower half from the eastern upper half. The Saw Mill River Parkway borders the eastern half, while the western half borders on Saw Mill River Road, where all of the entrances are located.

It is rumored that three women dressed in white haunt the cemetery. They mainly linger near a hill at the center of the cemetery, which is lined

This unmarked crypt is the final resting place of Elisha G. Otis.

by the graves of children. At night, these ghostly women in white have been said to chase trespassers away from the hill and out of the cemetery. Sometimes you can feel a presence around you while in the cemetery. It is as if you are being watched. Footsteps have been heard, and photos of misty apparitions have been captured near the hill where these spirits are said to appear.

No one knows the identity of these three women. One rumor I heard was about them being the same three women who were either hanged or burned at the stake for witchcraft on Buckout Road in White Plains between the 1600s and 1800s. After extensive research, I found this possibility unlikely.

There has never been any documentation indicating that anyone was ever burned at the stake for witchcraft anywhere in the United States, including in Salem, Massachusetts. That was a common punishment during the European witch trials. Instead, it is possible they could have been hanged. Regardless, if these women were killed at Buckout Road, it would be an unnecessarily long journey to move three dead bodies from Buckout Road all the way down to Yonkers in a time when there were no cars and barely any roads. Why go through the trouble of traveling so far by horse and carriage to hide the bodies when it would be far easier to bury these alleged witches near Buckout Road, which is still surrounded by woodlands to this day?

There are cemeteries in the area that are much closer. One belonged to the Buckhout family, while another was meant for slaves. Any of those locations would have been ideal to bury three so-called witches, *if* this incident ever occurred.

During my first few visits to the cemetery, I noticed how many of the tombstones were knocked over. It's quite unfortunate how people can have such disrespect for the dead. It comes as no surprise the cemetery is under the protection of these angry spirits.

I later learned that there are some cemeteries that purposely lay down wobbly tombstones to avoid possible injury. The responsibility to pay for the stones to be reset falls on the relatives of the deceased. If there are no relatives or friends who can pay for the stone to be reset, it is very likely the stone will remain flat on the ground. At least, this is a practice that has been known to occur in New York City.

In late 2006, shortly after creating my team, I began doing paranormal investigations at this cemetery. During my first investigation here, I took a photograph of what appears to be three misty apparitions. The photo

I captured this image of what appears to be several smoky apparitions near the foot of a hill at Oakland Cemetery in 2006.

was taken at the approximate location where the three ghostly women are supposed to haunt. My EMF meter beeped once mere seconds before the photo was taken. I only took the photo because my teammate Chris said he felt a presence in that area.

I returned to the cemetery the next day with a different team member, Meagan. This time it was during the daytime. We checked the area where I captured the misty apparitions in the photo. Most of the graves in that area belonged to children.

It made me wonder. Maybe it was the three women who were watching over the graves of the children and letting us know they were there. When they realized we weren't vandals, maybe they left us alone.

Not too long afterward, we returned at night. After wrapping up our investigation, we started heading for the exit. All of a sudden, we heard distinct footsteps following behind us, crunching the leaves and fallen twigs. There was no wind or breeze on that night. As far as we could tell, no animals could be seen in the area. I actually stopped to search all around us with a very powerful LED flashlight to be sure.

Yet as soon as we resumed walking, the unmistakable sound of footsteps continued to follow us until we reached the exit. We could tell we were being watched, too. My teammates and I felt a strong presence.

Most of my teammates know that I rarely ever feel the presence of spirits around us during our investigations. I usually rely on the equipment we have to provide proof, so I tend to be a little more skeptical when the equipment shows no signs of paranormal activity. However, on that night, I felt something for the first time, and I knew we were not alone. Whatever we felt did not want us there. It's a good thing we were leaving anyway.

One of my teammates got so scared because of that experience that she never returned with us to Oakland Cemetery. She eventually left the team after she believed there were ghosts following her back home from our investigations.

Normally, I enjoy spending my time at cemeteries. It doesn't matter if it's day or night. I find them to be very peaceful. Some are even quite beautiful, depending on the landscape and statuary. I especially love it when the grass has been freshly cut because it smells great. I believe it helps that I have a great deal of respect for the dead. I never disrespect their graves or their spirits. I can only hope they realize that and cooperate with us during our investigations.

OTIS ELEVATOR COMPANY

Elisha Graves Otis was an industrialist from Vermont who founded the Otis Elevator Company after moving to Yonkers in 1851. Prior to that, he worked as a doll maker and as a wagon builder. While he may not have invented the elevator, which had already been around since the days of ancient Egypt, what he did invent would soon change the way of the world for centuries to follow.

Upon his arrival in Yonkers, Elisha found work as the manager of an old abandoned sawmill, which he was supposed to renovate into a bedstead factory. During the clean-up process, he was stumped as to how he could get the debris to the upper levels of the factory easily. He opted against the use of a hoisting platform because they were known to break and it was not worth the risk.

In 1852, together with his two sons, he designed a special type of safety elevator, which used a certain type of cog that was capable of stopping an elevator safely after only a few feet of movement. By 1853, Elisha had completed his invention, which he and his sons tested successfully. Once they realized it worked, they proceeded to move the debris to the upper levels without a second thought.

Prior to the creation of this new cog, elevator rides were sometimes known to end in disastrous falls, which limited their use significantly.

Neither Elisha nor his sons even considered the idea of getting a patent on their creation. It wasn't until the bedstead factory went under that he considered opening an elevator factory to sell his product. At first, the new company

A photo of Elisha G. Otis. *Courtesy of the Yonkers Historical Society.*

was called Union Elevator Works. It was later changed to Otis Brothers and Company and then to Otis Elevator Works. Finally, it became the Otis Elevator Company. Business was very slow for the first few months, but that was about to change.

Otis did a public demonstration for his invention at the Crystal Palace during the 1854 World's Fair in New York City. It was an instant success. Orders came in from all around the world, and he was forced to build a factory that could fulfill these orders. His invention would usher in a new era of skyscrapers, which was not possible before. This would forever change the landscape and skylines of nearly every major city in the world.

The first factory building of the Otis Elevator Company, located on Vark Street, was built with sturdy floors and high ceilings to support the heavy machinery and weight of the elevators built. Metal railings across the ceilings were used to move the elevators around within the factory. Each component went through extensive testing before being shipped out.

At one time, the Otis Elevator Company was one of the leading factories in the eastern United States. The factory complex stretched from Larkin Plaza to Ashburton Avenue and from Woodworth Avenue to the Hudson River. It was conveniently located near the New York Central Railroad tracks, which allowed for the easy distribution and transportation of parts

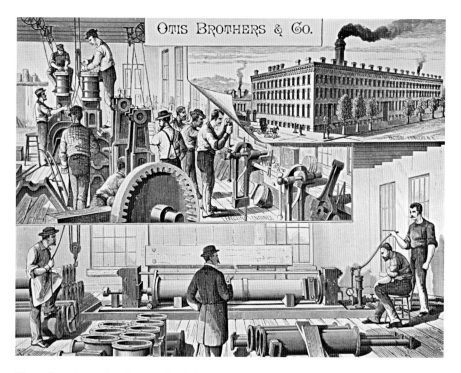

Shown here is an advertisement for Otis Brothers & Co. from the late 1800s. *Courtesy of the Yonkers Historical Society.*

The NY Zouave Artillery Co. in front of the original factory for Otis Steam Elevator Works, circa 1860. *Courtesy of the Yonkers Historical Society.*

into New York City. With a great demand for elevators across the world, the company continued to expand, becoming one of the largest employers in Yonkers for many decades.

When Elisha G. Otis died on April 8, 1861, he was interred in a family crypt at Oakland Cemetery in Yonkers. A small statuette of a doll sits on the steps in front of the crypt in memory of his time as a doll maker.

On March 31, 1889, the Eiffel Tower in Paris, France, was completed, equipped with Otis elevators. The French originally wanted to use French or European elevators, but the Otis Elevators Company was the only company in the entire world that could do the job required. The opening of the tower was delayed by a few weeks while the Otis Elevator Company installed the towers' elevators.

In July 1943, a malfunctioning metallurgical baking oven in one of the processing plants belonging to the Otis Elevator Company exploded. The explosion could be felt within a ten-block radius. Police arrived immediately, since the police station was only about a block away. The curious crowds also gathered quickly. Luckily, there was no fire and no injuries to report. There was only a huge cloud of smoke.

In 1976, the United Technologies Corporation of Hartford acquired the Otis Elevator Company. In turn, the Otis Elevator Company bought Evan Lifts Ltd., located in the United Kingdom. Evan Lifts Ltd. is the oldest manufacturer of lift equipment in the United Kingdom, and up until that time, it was also the largest. The Otis Customer Care Center is located within the old Evan Lifts building in Leicester, England. There are still Evan Lifts being used today.

The Otis Elevator Company closed its plant in Yonkers in 1982 due to rising costs. The buildings were sold to the Port Authority of New York and New Jersey. By 1983, the company vacated the old factory and relocated to North Carolina. Today, its main headquarters is based in Farmington, Connecticut.

One of the former Otis buildings in Yonkers is now home to the Yonkers Riverfront Library and the Yonkers Board of Education, while the Kawasaki Rail Car Company occupies the former elevator factory. Recently, an innovative American digital applications company named Mindspark has also made its home in a former Otis building.

Since moving to Yonkers during the 1980s, the Kawasaki Rail Car Company has built over 2,500 train cars. The company manufactures stainless steel trains for the New York City Transit Authority, the Long Island Railroad, Metro North Railroad and Port Authority Trans-Hudson

An aerial view taken during the early 1900s shows the signs atop the Otis Elevator Company's many buildings. *Courtesy of the Yonkers Historical Society.*

(PATH), and its trains can be found in Virginia, Maryland and Boston, Massachusetts.

Considering how old these buildings are, it doesn't sound too outrageous when someone tells you they are haunted. In the past, there have been accidental injuries or deaths due to mishaps. Over the years, many people have passed through the doors of the old factory buildings. Some workers spent their entire lives working there and continue to return long after death. Perhaps Elisha Otis himself has returned, wondering what happened to his elevator factory.

I heard firsthand from a friend who used to work at the Kawasaki factory that the buildings are indeed haunted. He wasn't the only employee who believed the buildings to be haunted. Other employees also had unexplained experiences while working there. However, it is usually frowned upon to spread such stories, so the employees generally keep quiet about what they see or hear.

At night, strange noises can be heard within the old factory structure, whose lofty brick smokestack still bears the name "Otis" down its side. In addition, the Kawasaki Rail Car Company still utilizes old equipment

The smokestack on this former Otis Elevator building still says "Otis" on it.

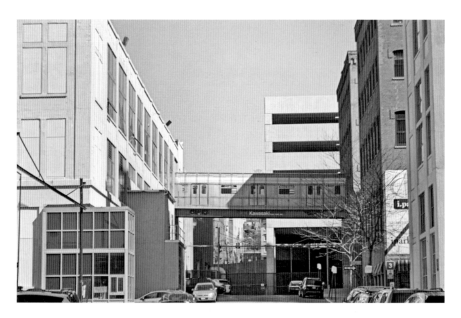

The "Kawasaki" name on this former Otis Elevator building is prominent on this bridge, which was made to look like a train car.

formerly used by Otis. It's possible residual energy from the past could have attached itself to the former Otis equipment and machinery. Photos of orbs have been captured within the old warehouse. Several employees have also reported seeing apparitions roaming around.

One apparition that has been seen is an old gentleman who is believed to have once worked in the building long before it was owned by the Kawasaki Rail Car Company.

Today, the Otis Elevator Company is the world's largest manufacturer of vertical transportation systems. The company mainly focuses on elevators and escalators and has installed elevators in some of the world's most famous structures, which include New York's Empire State Building and former World Trade Center buildings, Disney's Twilight Zone Tower of Terror ride, the Petronas Twin Towers in Malaysia, Ontario's CN and Skylon Towers, the luxurious Hotel del Coronado in San Diego, the "Pizza Elevator" at Lake Point Tower in Chicago and so many more.

In October 2013, the Otis Elevator Company won what has become its biggest ever contract, which is to supply 670 elevators and escalators to the Hyderabad Metro Rail in India.

PHILIPSE MANOR HALL

Philipse Manor Hall is the oldest house in Yonkers, as well as in all of Westchester County. Built from 1680 to 1682 by Frederick Philipse, a wealthy Dutchman of Bohemian heritage, it's located on Warburton Avenue at Larkin Plaza. During its early years, it was essentially the center of the city. Philipse resided there with his wife, Margaret Hardenbroeck, and their children.

Frederick Philipse was born in Bolswaert, Friesland, in 1626. His first land holding in New Netherlands was in New Amsterdam. It was a lot he acquired in 1658 located on the northeast corner of the Markveld (Market Field) and Brouwer Straat, which is now the corner of Whitehall and Stone Streets.

On November 29, 1672, Frederick Philipse purchased a large tract of land, which would someday become the Manor of Philipsburgh. The land originally belonged to Adriaen van der Donck, founder of Yonkers, but it was passed on to his widow after his death. She sold it soon afterward to her brother, and he sold it off one section at a time. Philipse was one of the buyers. His initial purchase was made in partnership with two other men, Thomas Lewis and Thomas Delaval.

By this time, there was a very prosperous business at the mill near the mouth of the Nepperhan River, which would someday be renamed as the Saw Mill River. Philipse knew business would only get better as time went on. In 1680, he began construction on his new home in the downtown area of Yonkers. He chose a location close to the mill near the river's edge.

The heavy south door of the house was handcrafted in Holland and shipped overseas to the Netherlands within the same year, along with many bricks from Holland, via one of Philipse's sailing ships. In 1681, he began to add more land to his growing estate by buying out one of his partners. His home was completed in 1682, although a west wing was added sometime between 1682 and 1694. By 1686, he bought out his other partner and had become the sole owner of the land.

A year earlier, in 1685, Philipse built the Old Dutch Church in Sleepy Hollow. This historic church has been featured in Washington Irving's legendary tale, *The Legend of Sleepy Hollow*. It is still standing today and is one of the oldest churches in New York. Behind it is one of the oldest burial grounds in Westchester County. This church also happens to be where I married my wife on May 4, 2014.

Across the road from the church, Philipse built another house, which has become a historic site known as Philipsburg Manor. The site includes a gristmill and a barn, replicas of the kind that once stood on the land. This home was commonly referred to as the Upper Mill, while the Manor Hall was referred to as the Lower Mill.

The left image shows the Manor Hall in 1682. The right image shows how it looked prior to 1745. *Courtesy of the Yonkers Historical Society.*

Philipse Manor, circa 1784. *Courtesy of the Yonkers Historical Society.*

Along the riverbanks of the Hudson, Philipse grew grain, which was then ground into flour at his mills. The finished product was later transported via one of his ships to ports around the world.

After his first wife, Margaret, died in 1692, Philipse remarried. His second wife, Catherine, was the daughter of the Honorable Oloff Stevenzen Van Cortlandt. Their union brought him additional prestige, which allowed him to make new business and financial connections.

On June 12, 1693, the Manor of Philipsburgh, or Philipsborough Manor, was created by way of a royal charter. This would mark the beginning of a new era in the history of the newly formed Westchester County. It was also around this time that Yonkers became a township with the new Philipse Manor Hall as its seat of government. It was only a matter of time before the Manor Hall became the civic and social center for pretty much the entire Lower Hudson River Valley.

Within the same year, Philipse erected a toll bridge that would cross the Spuyten Duyvil Creek, connecting Manhattan Island to the Manor of Philipsburgh. The bridge, which he named King's Bridge, would be the only means of crossing by foot or horse for many years, until the addition of another bridge that became known as the Farmers' Free Bridge because it did not have a toll. The creek was later filled in, making both bridges redundant. This area later became known as Kingsbridge Heights.

In 1694, Philipse added more property to his estate when he purchased fifty acres of land at George Point in Yonkers from Matthys Janszen Buckhout. By this time, Philipse owned about 156,000 acres of land, which spread over a distance of nearly twenty-one miles. It essentially made up the entire western half of Westchester County going from the Spuyten Duyvil Creek at the northern end of Manhattan up to the Croton River. Philipse even owned a small portion of land on the New Jersey side of the Hudson River.

There were many tenants residing within the Manor of Philipsburgh. Most were farmers. Rent days were held twice a year at both the Lower and Upper Mills. The rent paid depended mainly on the value of the land leased by the tenant. Sometimes it would be paid in hens or bushels of wheat. Rent days were generally enjoyable social events and seemed more like parties. The lord of the manor saw to it that his tenants were provided with a fine dinner, while the tenants used the opportunity to socialize with one another and exchange gossip.

Philipse was a businessman, and his main business was the slave trade. He made more money from slave trading than he did from any other business endeavor. Between the years 1685 and 1698 alone, he made at least six slave trade journeys from Africa to both Europe and the Americas.

The slaves were mainly collected from Africa. During these journeys, they were stored like cargo in coffin-like wooden boxes. That's where they would remain for the duration of the long sea voyage. These boxes are essentially where they lived. They slept in them, sat in them and ate meals there, and whenever they had to use the bathroom, it was also in the boxes. They were rarely allowed out of their boxes during the entire trek across the Atlantic.

While at Philipse Manor Hall, my wife and I had the opportunity to lie inside similar boxes that are on display on the museum's first floor. It was a very tight, uncomfortable fit. I cannot imagine spending more than a few minutes in one of those boxes, let alone traveling across the expanse of the Atlantic Ocean on a wooden sailing ship as a slave with no freedom to leave that box.

Of the more than one hundred slaves transported during each crossing, there would usually be a loss of around 10 percent of them. This was to be expected, due to the extreme harshness of the journey. Other slaves would usually be ordered to toss the dead slaves overboard into the sea. Philipse had certain slaves working on the ships in order to help out.

Both the slave trade business and the ownership of the Manor of Philipsburgh, including the Manor Hall, were passed down from generation to generation within the family, as was the name of Frederick Philipse.

Upon Philipse's death in 1702, the manor went to his son, Adolph, who built up the manor during his ownership. However, it was Philipse's second wife, Lady Catherine, who was the life and the light of the Manor Hall. Church records describe her as being tenderly spoken, prudent and very wise. She was well loved by the people. She died in 1730.

My wife and I lying within the same types of coffin-like boxes used to transport slaves aboard ships. *Photo taken by Richard Embree.*

Sometime during the early 1740s, a new wing was added just north of the entrance. In 1755, the north wing was extended to its current size.

By 1750, when Adolph died, the tenant population increased from two hundred to over one thousand. With no will left behind, it was Adolph's nephew, Frederick Philipse II, who inherited the manor. He only owned it for one year before it was passed on to his son, Frederick Philipse III.

Prior to the American Revolutionary War, Frederick Philipse III had a daughter with his wife. For a brief period of time, a young soon-to-be-famous man by the name of George Washington courted their daughter, whose name was Mary. However, the young couple was not meant to be and did not marry.

Instead, Mary married Washington's friend, Roger Morris, in the winter of 1758. The wedding was held within the manor's southeast Rococo Parlor on the first floor. During the ceremony, a Native American wrapped in a crimson blanket appeared unannounced. The intruder brought with him a gloomy prediction for the family. He foresaw the inevitable downfall of the Philipse family and essentially the end of British colonial rule in America. The Philipse family disregarded the prophet as a delusional savage, and his warnings went ignored.

Interestingly, Mary Philipse and Roger Morris built their home in what would someday become the Morris-Jumel Mansion, located in the Washington Heights section of Manhattan. After the Revolutionary War, their home became known as George Washington's headquarters because he used it as such during the early part of the war. It stands today as a museum and is one of the most haunted locations in Upper Manhattan.

This portrait of Frederick Philipse III can be seen hanging within Philipse Manor Hall. *Courtesy of Philipse Manor Hall.*

Frederick Philipse III was a prominent Loyalist, loyal to the British Crown. This would ultimately prove to be his undoing, making him the last lord of the Manor of Philipsburgh. Only months after the colonists signed the Declaration of Independence in 1776, over two hundred Loyalists met at the Manor Hall to sign their own Declaration of Dependence. They had sealed their own fate by signing that declaration, along with that of the Philipse family, as predicted.

When the colonists won the war for independence in 1783, Frederick Philipse III was branded a traitor and arrested on orders signed by General George Washington himself. Philipse was taken to New Rochelle, where he was confined under guard for eleven days. He was sent to Connecticut and given parole, although he was given special permission to return to Yonkers to get his affairs in order. Instead, he and his family fled the newly freed colonies and escaped to England.

As a direct result, in 1785, Philipse Manor Hall and the entire Manor of Philipsburgh were subsequently confiscated by the State of New York. The Philipse steward, John Williams, remained to watch over the house. The Commissioners of Forfeiture then sold off the land to sixty-four different families, which mainly consisted of tenant farmers who wished to own the land their families had toiled over for generations.

Frederick Philipse III died the same year, while in England. The Philipse family members who fled were forever banished from the state. In the event of their return, they would be found guilty of a felony and sentenced to death.

The Manor Hall was sold at a public auction and passed through a series of owners during the first half of the nineteenth century. By the 1840s, a farmer named Lemuel W. Wells owned it. He used it as a boarding house.

While engineer Thomas C. Cornell was working on the Hudson River Railroad Line at around the same time, he rented out an office within the Manor Hall. After completing his section of the railroad in 1849, he settled at Yonkers. He continued to rent a room at the Manor Hall for a short time afterward, until he found a more suitable place to live.

Wells sold the Manor Hall to William W. Woodworth during the same year. Woodworth was a former judge and congressman, as well as being a principal contractor on the Yonkers portion of the railroad.

On January 14, 1864, President Abraham Lincoln sent a letter to Yonkers in regard to the village's forthcoming Sanitary Fair, which was held a month later during the third week of February. The letter is currently on display on the second floor of the Manor Hall in the Gothic Chamber.

In 1868, the Village of Yonkers used the Manor Hall as its village hall. When Yonkers became a city in 1872, it became its city hall. It continued to serve as such for the next few decades.

Between 1891 and 1892, the Civil War Soldiers and Sailors Monument was built on the front lawn to honor the men who served during the war. This towering monument, which was paid for by citizens of Yonkers, is flanked on two sides by actual cannons and cannon balls left over from the Spanish-American War. The figures on the monument represent an infantryman, a marine, a sailor, a cavalryman and the standard bearer, which is holding a flag and standing high atop the obelisk. There are also quotations engraved around the base taken from famous people in history, such as President Abraham Lincoln.

On January 28, 1902, Mayor Michael J. Walsh appointed a committee to negotiate the sale of the Manor Hall and its grounds to the State of New York for historical purposes. A joint meeting was held, in which it was decided the American Scenic and Historic Preservation Society was more suitable to acquire said property. In addition, the city government was committed to the preservation of the Manor Hall for historic purposes until it could be compensated for giving up the use of its grounds for municipal purposes.

Philipse Manor Hall prior to the erection of the war memorial, circa 1870, by H.S. Wyer. *Wikipedia.*

A year later, legislature introduced a bill for the State of New York to purchase the Manor Hall for the sum of $50,000, although the property was worth much more. When the bill was not passed, it was later reintroduced in 1904 and again in 1905 without success.

On October 16, 1907, the Civic League of Woman's Institute held a meeting to discuss the future of the Manor Hall. During the meeting, it was suggested the group reach out to a wealthy person of the community to help save the Manor Hall. By the next day, Eva Smith Cochran, the wealthiest woman in Yonkers at the time, agreed to donate the $50,000 needed. As a result, on January 7, 1908, the bill was finally passed, and the American Scenic and Historic Preservation Society became the custodian of the property.

Between 1908 and 1911, the municipal offices were gradually relocated from the Manor Hall to the new Beaux-Arts City Hall building, which had been built atop a hill in Washington Park at 40 South Broadway.

Extensive renovations were done on the Manor Hall between 1911 and 1912. When they were complete, the house had been brought back to its former colonial glory. Afterward, the aptly named Philipse Manor Hall opened as a museum and has remained one ever since.

In 1971, Philipse Manor Hall was closed for a period of five years so numerous repairs and restorations could be made. The structure had been deteriorating and was in great need of repairs. Restoration work included a new roof; the installation of new heating, plumbing and ventilation systems; and improvements on the ceilings and woodwork. Exhibits and paintings were professionally treated, while new exhibits were also added. By July 1976, Philipse Manor Hall was finally ready to reopen, in time for the bicentennial.

Considering how many centuries it has been around, it isn't too hard to believe there are stories about it being haunted. People have seen apparitions walking through the old hall. At night when the hall is empty, there have been reports of someone seen through the windows walking around holding a candle. One staff member witnessed the apparition of a male in broad daylight as he stood in front of a window of the Gothic Chamber. The apparition was wearing gold-colored pantaloons and a vest over a ruffled shirt. Staff members have also heard disembodied voices and footsteps while they were alone. There have even been reports of unexplained foul odors, although that is probably not paranormal in nature. The motion detector sometimes goes off for no reason. One person from a paranormal team has even claimed a spirit possessed her while conducting a paranormal investigation at night.

Is it possible the ghost of Frederick Philipse III haunts the home he was forced to flee so many years ago, trying to claim in death what he could no longer have in life?

After learning of all the activity said to have taken place at Philipse Manor Hall, a paranormal team named the New York Ghost Chapter (NYGC) conducted a paranormal investigation on the premises. They were able to capture several EVP recordings and a few photos with orbs in them. They asked questions and got back answers, such as "We watch" and "Please, go away."

For those who are unaware, EVP stands for "electronic voice phenomena." It's basically when an unknown unexplainable voice that appears to be caused by a spirit is captured on an electronic recording device.

Philipse Manor Hall, as it appears today, with the war memorial to the far left in the foreground.

On August 1, 2013, I conducted a paranormal investigation at the location with my team. We had the place to ourselves since it was empty, aside from the security guard. It was a perfect opportunity to capture an EVP. Unfortunately, we did not collect any evidence at all.

However, something odd occurred when we first arrived on that rainy afternoon. As we approached the main entrance, a middle-aged male visitor was just leaving with his female companion. He looked directly into my eyes and said, "This place is clean," as if he knew why I was there. He then walked away without another word. Naturally, I found it rather strange that he would even think to say this to me, although by the time I left, I was inclined to agree.

One fascinating secret few people know of is that when the manor was built, an underground tunnel leading to the Hudson River was added. It is likely the Philipse family used this tunnel when they fled for England. I am unsure whether this tunnel is still accessible, but I would imagine it was built under the oldest part of the house. I've been down to the basement and did not find a tunnel, although there is brick archway directly under the fireplace of the West Parlor that leads nowhere.

I wouldn't be surprised if the tunnel was sealed up long ago to prevent trespassers and thieves from sneaking into the museum. It's unknown

This brick archway located in the basement beneath the West Parlor may very well have been the entrance to a tunnel leading to the river.

exactly where the other end of the tunnel exited, but I'm sure it was sealed up as well.

Philipse Manor Hall was designated a National Historic Landmark in 1961. Five years later, it was added to the National Register of Historic Places.

The original key to the front door was safely locked away, but the Yonkers Historical Society has since adopted its symbol as its emblem. The original key is the oldest known key in all of Westchester County. Duplicates of this centuries-old key are occasionally awarded to people as the society's esteemed "Key to History" award. At this writing, the most recent recipient was my friend Angelique Piwinski, who received the award on November 2, 2014.

PUBLIC SCHOOL 6

Public School 6, once located on Ashburton Avenue between North Broadway and Warburton Avenue, was designed and built by architect C.C. Chipman sometime in the 1890s. Chipman had also designed a number of other school buildings throughout Yonkers. This three-story brick building had a fabulous stone archway over its entrance that seemingly welcomed children into its doors for many years.

A closer look into the politics of this educational establishment told a different tale. Children of black and Latino descent were not so welcomed in this particular school. Racism was still quite alive in Yonkers during the 1980s. However, after an integration lawsuit proved the city was unlawfully segregating the children allowed into this school, it marked the end of an era for local residents. In 1986, the school was permanently closed, and its students were integrated into other local schools.

For the children who attended the school and didn't understand the reasoning behind why it closed, it was a confusing and disappointing time. Friendships were lost, as they were forced to make new beginnings elsewhere. It's not easy for a child to start over mid-semester. Surely, a few educations suffered because of the sudden change.

In time, the windows were boarded up and a fence was erected around the building to prevent anyone from entering. For nearly two decades afterward, the school was abandoned and virtually forgotten. In some ways, it was a

Public School 6 in 1906. *Courtesy of the Yonkers Historical Society.*

Public School 6, as it appeared during the early 2000s. *Courtesy of Rob Yasinsac (www. hudsonvalleyruins.org).*

bad reminder for the community, so it was easy to forget about it. By the 2000s, the roof began to cave in, which resulted in a partial roof collapse sometime around the early part of 2007.

The fence and boarded-up windows did little to keep trespassers out. If someone wants to enter bad enough, they will. Sure enough, it became a haven for the homeless, drug addicts, gangs, urban explorers and would-be ghost hunters.

It was also rumored to be haunted. Considering it was a darkened old building on the middle of a lonely hill, it certainly had the look of a haunted location. I honestly couldn't tell you any of the claims made in regard to this location because I have not heard any specific ghost stories, aside from hearsay from reliable sources. I only remember driving past it and wondering to myself if it were indeed haunted. To my knowledge, no one has ever died on the property in such a way that would cause any kind of haunting—not that a death is required for a haunting. Sometimes spirits just can't let go of their past.

Unfortunately, I never had the opportunity to conduct a paranormal investigation at the location either, much to my regret. I would have at least liked to get a look at the interior, while it was abandoned.

I had no idea why it was abandoned until I began researching for this book. It's a shame a school would have to be shut down due to segregation. You would think we left those awful experiences far behind us.

I was just starting high school when this school closed in 1986. As a Puerto Rican, I am grateful throughout my educational years growing up in the Bronx that I never had to experience any kind of segregation. I spent most of my school years in honors classes, so I was generally surrounded by students who wanted to learn and were good at it. My teachers all seemed like good-hearted, fair people. I believe they genuinely cared about their students. I still look back fondly on many of my memories of them and give them due credit for the educated and accomplished person I have become.

When Public School 6 was closed for good, it was probably for the best. Of course, I'm sure its former students would disagree. It wasn't about politics or segregation for them. It was simply their school and a place where they made friends and built memories.

There were originally plans to raze the building and use the land for commercial redevelopment in the early 2000s, but those plans fell through and the building was left standing a few years longer. It was ultimately demolished sometime after 2011. The new plan was to build apartment buildings on the site. A new structure already stands in its place using the original archway, but for the former students of Public School 6, that archway will always be a haunting part of their childhood memories.

SAINT JOSEPH'S CEMETERY

Saint Joseph's Cemetery was established in 1876. Situated at the northern tip of Yonkers, bordering Tompkins Avenue, its main entrance is located on Truman Avenue. The oldest grave I found here dates back to 1856, belonging to a man buried with a woman who died in 1872. Both are dated prior to the establishment of the cemetery. There are also soldiers buried here who died during the American Civil War.

This area was once known as Nepera Park. During the early to mid-1800s, there was a farm on the site that belonged to an old Yonkers firm called Wells, Miller and Provost, Canners and Producers. At the time, it specialized in growing cucumbers and other vegetables, producing pickles and then canning them at a processing plant for the purpose of selling them. The plant was located farther south on Nepperhan Avenue, just past Odell Avenue.

The owner of the farm, John Wells, resided in a large house that is still standing on Nepperhan Avenue across from the entrance to Truman Avenue. It used to be known as the "White House," although it is no longer white. The once beautiful veranda surrounding the house has been enclosed in stucco, taking away from its original ranch-like appearance.

Wells, Miller and Provost did quite well for a while until two separate devastating fires destroyed processing plants in Atlanta, Georgia, and in nearby Harriman, New York. The firm was unable to recover financially from the combined aftermath of both fires. It was then that the farm was passed on to the Austin family. Daniel Austin, who purchased the farm and processing plant, had been a foreman for the company. He carried on the business with the help of his son, Willsey. Together, they continued the tradition of making pickles, for which their family became well known.

By 1900, the pickle industry in Westchester began to suffer. It marked the end of the Austin Pickle Farm. By 1903, the last Austin left the farm, and soon Nepperhan Avenue was extended onto their former land. The cemetery was also expanded until it reached Tompkins Avenue.

This cemetery holds a special place in my heart. It was the site of my first two paranormal investigations. On the first night in November 2006, I was not disappointed. While standing at the northeast corner on Nepperhan Avenue, I acquired my first ghostly photo of an apparition within minutes of being there. It appeared to be a young woman in a dress with her shoulders exposed, who was hovering approximately five feet over the graves. I noticed her right away in one photo. By the time I took another, she was gone. I was with my cousin Christina at the time.

I can only imagine we aroused the curiosity of the spirits by being there at night. Perhaps this female apparition was coming to take a closer look at us, or maybe she was trying to communicate with us. I only wish I had my tape recorder with me, but I did not think about it until it was too late.

We returned the next night with our cousin Meagan. This time we came prepared. I brought along my old tape recorder and turned it on right away. At some point, I had to tell my cousins to quiet down because they were joking around and making fun of one of the names on a tombstone.

Apparently, they managed to offend the spirits because at that moment, we saw a smoky apparition rise up from a nearby tombstone. I immediately

The apparition of a woman wearing a strapless dress to the far left was captured during my first investigation at St. Joseph's Cemetery in 2006.

took a photo and successfully captured the image, which to this day it is one of my best photos of an apparition. It appears to have wings and multiple faces, including a human skull. We all saw it, and it gave us a chill. At the same time, we were also able to capture an EVP from this apparition on the tape recorder, as it made a moaning sound.

My cousins promptly realized this was not a game we were playing. They apologized to the spirits and learned the importance of respecting the dead.

The electromagnetic activity in that area is quite high, especially along the rows of graves closer to Nepperhan Avenue. However, they are directly beneath power lines, which run along the sidewalk.

Still, these early paranormal experiences were enough inspiration for me to continue doing paranormal investigations with my team, the Yonkers Ghost Investigators.

I had an interesting experience here with my former team member Giselle. Shortly after entering the cemetery, she felt something touch her arm. I figured it might have been a spider web, although it seemed unlikely since there was nowhere it could cling to on one side. We were walking along one of the paths.

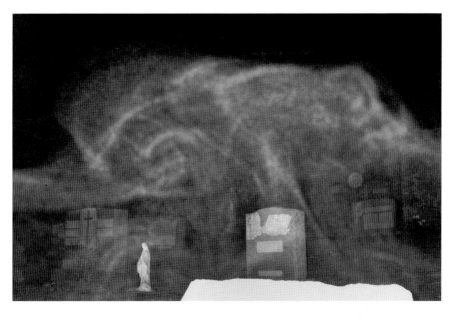

During our second investigation, I captured this disturbing image of an apparition just as it rose up from the tombstone in front of me.

My nephew and fellow paranormal investigator Chris Gonzalez checks the electromagnetic energy levels using an EMF meter.

Spirits have touched people more than once in this cemetery, myself included. There are cobweb-like sensations felt in areas where there are no spider webs. This is generally considered to be a sensation associated with the touch of a ghost.

As Giselle and I proceeded north, we gradually made our way toward the back of the cemetery. Soon we reached a set of old graves on the hill at the western edge that border the woods. I started taking photos, until we heard what sounded like footsteps approaching. We thought it was coming from the woods. It could have been an animal. I really don't know, but I was alert and ready. I handed the camera to Giselle, and she took over taking photos, while I checked the perimeter around us.

She began taking a series of about twenty photographs in a row, which all contained what appears to be a misty apparition. She also felt a presence around us, and it showed in every photo she took in the form of a white apparition. It seemed like the apparition was becoming more and more apparent with each photo. I even wiped the lens twice to make sure it was clean. It still kept showing up even brighter than before.

All of a sudden, the misty apparition was gone. We continued taking photos, but there was nothing out of the ordinary. Giselle could no longer feel a presence around us, either. Whatever was there with us had left abruptly. We also left soon afterward, having gathered enough evidence to satisfy us for one night.

During another night investigation with a former teammate, Melissa Mezo, we went to visit the grave of her grandfather. She attempted to communicate with him using a digital voice recorder. When we got home and listened to the recording, she was shocked to hear a deep male voice that said, "The shed...empty."

Melissa contacted me and told me about the EVP she captured. It didn't make a lot of sense to her for him to say what was said. However, what I learned next made it all too clear for me.

My father informed me that our former next-door neighbor, Henry, was buried there when he died in the early 2000s. When my father told me exactly where Henry was buried, I realized it was only a couple rows west from Melissa's grandfather.

After Henry died and his home was sold, the new resident tore down his old shed to make room for a personal basketball court. Henry used to enjoy spending warm days sitting out in his backyard near his shed. He'd often spend time in the shed, as well. Now it was gone. The ground where it once stood was empty.

I began to wonder, was it Henry speaking to me that night? I returned numerous times afterward and tried to communicate with him at his grave. As far as I know, I never got a response.

According to one of my other former team members, she saw a person walking a dog on the western hill and thought nothing of it. This was during the daytime, while visiting the grave of a family member with her mother. She turned away briefly to face her mother. When she looked back to the hill, she noticed the person with the dog had vanished. There was nowhere they could have gone that fast without being seen.

Shadows have also been seen moving around in the dark along the hills at the western edge of the cemetery. Strange, unexplained drawn-out screaming sounds have been heard in that area as well. While there are a lot of deer in the area, their cries sound very different from what we recorded. These screams don't sound like any wildlife that inhabit the area. We've compared them to several possible animals and birds but came up blank. These eerie screams can be heard by visiting the evidence section of our website. Over the years, there have been many EVPs recorded throughout the cemetery by my team.

In my opinion, this location remains one of the biggest hotspots for paranormal activity in Yonkers. If you are looking for ghosts, you might want to pay this place a visit. Just make sure they don't follow you back home! These spirits have a tendency to do so. Also, keep in mind that it is illegal to trespass in the cemetery at night, and you can be prosecuted if you are caught. I don't advise breaking the law to anyone.

Saint Joseph's Seminary

Saint Joseph's Seminary is located on Seminary Avenue in the Dunwoodie section of Yonkers. It's just north of Yonkers Avenue, high atop Valentine Hill, overlooking the Cross County Parkway and much of Yonkers. When one looks at the grand beauty of the seminary, it's easy to forget how the land might have been before its construction. In fact, the land where it was built is quite rich with colonial history.

In colonial times, the land, much like the rest of Yonkers, was part of the Manor of Philipsburgh. In 1720, a man by the name of Matthias Valentine became a tenant of the manor and leased out the land. He erected a typical colonial farmhouse on the summit of the hill near the northwest corner of the "Mile Square," which today is Mile Square Road.

During the American Revolutionary War, General George Washington stayed on the Valentine property as a guest of Thomas Valentine, the son of Matthias, for a total of two days in late October 1776. This was following his retreat from New York City, while on his way to White Plains. The site was chosen particularly for its strategic view over the Bronx River Valley, the Tibbetts Brook Valley and the Long Island Sound. This elevated position would allow them to easily watch for the movement of British troops.

On October 21, 1776, Washington was standing with Valentine in front of the farmhouse when he spotted British troops on a hill across the Bronx River Valley, in what is now Mount Vernon. He immediately rallied his troops and moved them northward to White Plains, traveling over Mile Square Road to Tuckahoe Road and then through Aquehung and the Tuckahoe Hills over to the Bronx River Road. He made his way north into White Plains, where the Battle of White Plains would later be fought.

Throughout the war, Washington's army continued to use the farm on Valentine Hill as a temporary headquarters. It was even where the Continental army mustered at the start of the war.

Legend has it that during the war, colonists beheaded a Hessian soldier and then disposed of his head by throwing it down an old well somewhere on the farm. This morbid tale was passed down for generations, and it came my way through the father of a friend, who grew up in Yonkers hearing of this urban legend.

While researching the story, I learned it is briefly mentioned in *Legends and Lore of Sleepy Hollow and the Hudson River Valley*, a book by well-known Sleepy Hollow historian Jonathan Kruk. In his book, Kruk mentions a "horrid specter with a bloody neck stump" that has been sighted in the neighborhood by no doubt regretful witnesses. He also says that the spirit was probably an unfortunate "Cowboy" who was captured and beheaded by rebels that were hell bent on revenge.

There were a few Loyalists to the British Crown who engaged in petty acts of thievery. These men were called "Cowboys" and sometimes "Refugees." They would usually raid local farmers and steal from them. If caught, they were generally hanged from a tree as punishment.

Incidentally, there were also Patriots who stole from the locals. These men were called "Skinners" because they more often stole clothing—in a sense, "skinning" their victims.

Given the two stories in regard to an alleged beheading, one must wonder if there actually was a person beheaded on Valentine Hill. While both versions of the legend differ in many ways, they both end with someone

General George Washington returns to the Valentine homestead, before moving on to Dobbs Ferry. *Image created by Tobitt-Punce and provided by the Yonkers Historical Society.*

being beheaded. That leaves me to conclude that someone was probably beheaded in the area, although the circumstances of how or why it happened remain a mystery.

Of course, I'm just guessing. Whether there is any truth to these tales is beyond my knowledge. In addition, I cannot say if the Valentine family was involved or had any knowledge of the event. I have no idea where any wells might have been on the property. It is possible this is just an urban legend with no truth to it. Either that, or the tale was confused with a similar story from Sleepy Hollow, in which a Hessian soldier was actually beheaded during the war.

I know for a fact that British general William Howe did send a company of 250 Hessian soldiers to the vicinity of Ward's Tavern in Eastchester after Washington's retreat from the Battle of Harlem. These forces were engaged and defeated by Washington's Continental army. By the end of the skirmish, 10 Hessians were killed and 2 were captured. It is not impossible to believe that one of the Hessians could have been beheaded at some point.

A few years later during the war in the summer of 1781, over five thousand French troops under the command of Jean-Baptiste Donatien de Vimeur, Comte de Rochambeau, set up camp in Yonkers. They remained in the area from July to August before heading to Yorktown, Virginia, to assist Washington's troops.

It is believed the French military chaplain, the abbé Robin, held the very first mass in the Dunwoodie Section on Sunday, July 22, of that same year. The mass was held for both French and American troops. Unfortunately, there is no true evidence to substantiate this alleged event, although it has been detailed in other books regarding the history of Yonkers.

After the war, all of the land belonging to the Philipse family was confiscated due to their loyalty to England and sold off to tenant farmers. It was around this time, in 1786, when Thomas Valentine was able to purchase the land back for his family at the bargain price of fifty dollars per acre. The farmhouse later became known as the "Revolutionary House" because of its ties to the war.

For about 170 years, the land was home to the Valentine family, and it was passed on from generation to generation. It was during this time period that the hill would eventually become known as Valentine Hill. Unfortunately, the "Revolutionary House" was torn down in 1840.

On March 6, 1890, Thomas' great-grandson Nathaniel Valentine sold the land to Archbishop Michael Corrigan for $64,146.77, which added up to over $1,000.00 per acre. Originally located in Troy, New York, it was decided the seminary would better serve everyone if it were moved closer to New York City. The archbishop chose Valentine Hill because of its wonderful elevated view and proximity to New York City.

A year later on Pentecost Sunday, May 17, 1891, the cornerstone was laid for the new seminary building. It was a huge event. It was anticipated that 150,000 spectators would attend. However, due to transportation issues, only about 80,000 showed up, although that is still a great deal of people. By September 1896, the first classes had begun with ninety-eight students.

In 1931, the Yonkers Chapter of the Westchester County Historical Society erected a memorial to George Washington in honor of his time spent on Valentine Hill during the American Revolutionary War. A large monument made of granite was built at the cost of $745. The Keskeskick Chapter of the Daughters of the American Revolution (DAR) gave a bronze plaque that contained an inscription, which was mounted on stone. The marker is located on the Seminary Avenue wall of the seminary.

In October 1985, Pope John Paul II visited the seminary. It has become a tradition for visiting cardinals to plant a tree on the grounds.

For over a century, Saint Joseph's Seminary has turned out many prominent graduates who have gone on to become cardinals, archbishops and priests.

An early 1900s photo of St. Joseph's Seminary. *Courtesy of the Yonkers Historical Society.*

Today, the seminary's graduates are religious leaders and workers in many churches around the world.

It is the major seminary for the Archdiocese of New York, and its primary mission is to educate and develop men for the priesthood in the Catholic Church. Once nicknamed the "West Point of Seminaries" due to its strict discipline and thorough educational process, it holds a notable reputation as one of the most prestigious and theologically orthodox Roman Catholic seminaries in the country.

Unfortunately, that also makes it pretty hard to conduct a paranormal investigation there. Trespassing is forbidden, and surveillance cameras watch over the property.

UNTERMYER PARK

Untermyer Park is located on North Broadway, which was once known as the Albany Post Road because it basically leads upstate to Albany. The park's main address is at 945 North Broadway. This thirteen-acre park is a wonderful paradise nestled away in the suburbs of Yonkers.

Aside from the founder of Yonkers, Adriaen van der Donck, and then the wealthy Philipse family, the next earliest known owner of the land where the park now stands was the Bolmer family. William Bolmer owned much of the area, but it was M.T. Bolmer who actually owned the area that would someday become Untermyer Park.

By 1842, the Croton Aqueduct was created to allow fresh water to flow from the Croton River down to New York City. Millions of gallons of water passed through these grounds via an underground conduit that was mostly made up of brick and stone. There were several pump houses built along the length of the trail. Two were built at the western edge of the Bolmer Estate.

In 1864, a wealthy hat manufacturer named John Thomas Waring purchased the land. He made a bundle selling hats during the American Civil War, which was fought from 1861 to 1865. Using a great deal of his funds, he paid an architect named John Davis Hatch to build a mansion at the cost of $225,000. It was constructed from 1868 to 1870. Upon seeing the finished product, Waring called the mansion Greystone, named for the gray stones used to build it.

John T. Waring's grandniece Edith F. Newman donated this photo of Greystone to the Yonkers Historical Society. *Courtesy of the Yonkers Historical Society.*

The imposing ninety-nine-room mansion was a vast symmetrical structure overlooking the Hudson River, the cliffs of the Palisades and the heart of the estate. It had a certain elegant yet gothic beauty about it that added to its prestige. At the time, it was the largest, most magnificent home in Yonkers.

Due to an unexpected failed business venture that resulted in financial losses in 1876, combined with the loss from the amount of money Waring used to build his fabulous estate, he found himself dealing with an unfortunate financial hardship. Much to his regret, he was forced to sell his beloved estate.

The estate was sold for $150,000 to former mayor of New York Samuel Jones Tilden in 1879. Tilden had lost the previous presidential election of 1876 to Rutherford B. Hayes by only one vote. He did not bother to run again. Instead, he chose to retire to his fabulous new estate and dedicated the rest of his days to beautifying it. He spent about $500,000 to build greenhouses and other structures on the estate.

Tilden went to the extreme to make his home appear more like a royal palace. Tiled corridors and Turkish carpets covered the floors within. The rooms were decorated with wonderfully carved wooden furniture. There were canopy beds, rare paintings, expensive clocks, statuary and other priceless artifacts. An army of servants tended to his every whim.

While living on the estate, Tilden purchased more land and expanded his property. A railroad station was added near the estate for convenience, which is now the Greystone Station, just off of Warburton Avenue. A winding carriage trail connected the rear gates at Warburton Avenue to the main entrance on North Broadway. Tilden also added several gardens, which he loved dearly. He resided at Greystone until his death on August 4, 1886.

President Grover Cleveland was one of many who came to pay their respects to Tilden at his funeral before his remains were transferred to New Lebanon, New York, where he was buried.

One of Samuel J. Tilden's favorite rooms was the library, which was filled with hundreds of books. Upon his death, at least twenty thousand items from his personal library were donated to the New York Public Library, becoming part of its core founding collection.

By 1899, Greystone became the property of Samuel Untermyer, a multimillionaire lawyer. Untermyer had a great love for flowers, which he inherited from his mother, Theresa. It gave him immense pleasure when it came to planning his gardens and decorating his greenhouses. During the early 1900s, he expanded and redesigned the estate, creating much of the fantastic gardens and scenery that exists today. It is believed he spent over $1 million in doing so.

Samuel J. Tilden in his library at Greystone. *Courtesy of the Yonkers Historical Society.*

After the death of the wealthy Eva Smith Cochran in 1909, Untermyer purchased her neighboring estate, which stood just next door to the north of his own. Her former home, Duncraggan, which was a gorgeous mansion in its own right, was converted into Untermyer's guesthouse.

On March 4, 1913, soon after President Woodrow Wilson won the presidential election, he received a visit at the White House from Untermyer, who was there on behalf of his law firm, Guggenheim, Untermyer and

Samuel Untermyer on April 14, 1932.
Courtesy of the Library of Congress.

Marshall. The reason for the visit was to blackmail the president for the sum of $40,000. Apparently, President Wilson had an affair with the wife of a colleague while teaching as a professor at Princeton University years earlier.

At the time, President Wilson did not have the money. Untermyer volunteered to pay the amount out of his own pocket to the woman, but only on the condition that the president promised to appoint a nominee recommended by Untermyer to the first available vacancy on the United States Supreme Court. This was a condition the president agreed to with great reluctance.

In 1915, Untermyer hired well-known European landscape designer William Welles Bosworth to design a beautiful Grecian garden with Persian and Roman influences. Bosworth had already done landscaping work for the Rockefeller family, so he probably came highly recommended. Bosworth would create a stunning walled garden for Untermyer. The walls would help block out the distracting noises from North Broadway, while giving the garden its privacy. Turrets would be built at each corner, overlooking the garden, as if it were a small fortress.

Bosworth created a garden with the help of Charles Leavit. By the time it was complete, it had its own amphitheater, a cross-shaped canal, two pergolas, several mythically inspired statues and a classical pavilion temple with marble columns that overlooked a reflecting pool. The floors of the pergolas, temple and reflecting pool were covered in white tiles designed with mosaic artwork. Lions' heads carved by Frederick G. Roth would spout out water into the pool and canal. Two sphinxes each perched atop two tall columns would stand watch over the entire garden.

Below the garden to the west is a very old large tree. The garden's original design included removing the tree to put another canal in its place, but Untermyer refused to cut this old tree down. It still stands today.

The long staircase leading down to the overlook was also added around this time, as both the stairs and overlook are not shown in a map from 1899. The stairs have been nicknamed the "1,000 Steps," although there are

The sphinxes watch over the walled garden like stoic guardians.

Looking toward the sphinxes of the walled garden with the pavilion on the left and the pergolas on either side of the sphinxes.

not really that many steps. The colored gardens would have been added afterward at each level.

The northern part of the estate, which formerly belonged to Cochran, featured a series of rose gardens that led to a five-level Italian vegetable garden. Along the carriage trail heading south was an enormous thirty-six-foot-diameter sundial made of living plants. It was the only living sundial in the world, although all traces of it are gone today.

Each Tuesday, the public was allowed to visit the gardens at no cost. Busloads of visitors would arrive at the estate each week, as people traveled for miles from other states, in order to view the wonderful gardens. Magazines did articles on the exquisite Untermyer gardens. This is why there are so many old photographs of the estate and its gardens in existence today. Untermyer took great pride in his gardens and wanted to share their beauty with the world. In September 1939, approximately thirty thousand spectators visited the park on one day.

Untermyer continued to add land to his estate and filled that land with more gardens and greenhouses. He was a lover of botany, although some of his gardens were rock gardens. He even had a "Temple of Love" gazebo imported from France for his daughter's wedding. It was placed on an aerie of rocks that was nicknamed the Eagle's Nest. It has six columns and an iron-laced cupola. A gentle waterfall would trickle down the rocks just below the small temple into a pond below.

From the Eagle's Nest, you can follow a stone walkway that takes you from the upper portion through a tunnel under the rocks to a balcony overlooking the pond below. It's almost like entering the gateway to a magical land. At the balcony, there is a stone staircase that leads down to the area where the pond is located.

Untermyer was very involved in politics. He had a lot of powerful friends and more than likely a few enemies, as well. He would later play a big role in trying to ease the economy during the Great Depression, while also declaring his own personal vendetta against Adolf Hitler and his Nazi party throughout the time of World War II, a crusade that would last until his death on March 16, 1940.

After his death, his property was willed to the City of Yonkers. Neither the state nor the county of Westchester wanted anything to do with it. It was simply too large and costly to maintain. The City agreed to take possession of the property on the condition it could sell part of it.

In 1946, Untermyer Park was opened to the public but with only forty-three acres of its former land. The portion of land that had once belonged

The Temple of Love at the Eagle's Nest, one of the elaborate rock gardens at the park. *Photo taken by Xavier Gonzalez using infrared photography.*

to the Cochran Estate and housed Duncraggan was sold and used to build a new hospital, Saint John's Riverside Hospital. A building at the hospital was actually named in Eva Smith Cochran's honor, due to her extensive efforts in funding the hospitals of Yonkers. There is still an original stone pillar of her estate located at the bus stop on North Broadway in front of the hospital, which says "Duncraggan."

Meanwhile, the new park next door did fine for its first two decades in existence. It was a suitable place for residents to enjoy a nice walk through the walled garden or along the old carriage trail. The gazebos and garden were the most popular spots for young couples and photographers. They remain so today.

Gradually, the grandeur of the park began to decline. The pool in the walled garden was drained between the 1940s and 1950s. The Greystone mansion was demolished in 1948 after it had fallen into a poor state of abandonment. It was ultimately replaced by the New York Cardiac Home, which was built between 1954 and 1955. It later became the Richmond Children's Center, and a playground was constructed over the area where the house once stood. Only the old stone railing remains, which once marked the boundary of the balconies that overlook the grounds. The once astounding view of the Hudson and Palisades has become largely obstructed by the growth of trees over the decades.

I'd like to think that if there were an active historical society at the time, it would have worked to save Greystone from destruction. As luck would have it, the city did not have a historical society throughout the 1940s. By the time a new one would emerge, it was too late.

By the 1960s, the park became a popular gathering location. Unfortunately, it also attracted undesirables. People would go there to get high or drunk. Sometimes they'd go up into the turrets of the garden to do so. At some point, the park had to install doors with locks to prevent addicts from entering the turrets. Most of the once beautiful locations were beginning to show signs of damage and decay. The waterfall near the Eagle's Nest was turned off at around this time.

For many years, the balcony beneath the Temple of Love gazebo overlooking the pond below did not have a railing, which made falling from there a constant danger for park visitors. Someone who used to frequent the park told me that someone did, in fact, fall and broke his neck in the process. Afterward, a metal railing was installed at the edge of the balcony for safety.

Following the Carriage Trail from that area will lead you to the Old Croton Aqueduct Trail. Soon you will come upon the old gatehouse, where

Four lion's head fountains spouted water from the curved wall beneath the pavilion into this once magnificent mosaic pool, which now lies in ruins.

the once majestic statues of a lion and unicorn guard the entrance. Sadly, the unicorn no longer has a head. No one seems to know when its head was destroyed. I have been unsuccessful in locating any photos of it with a head. As far as I can tell, there may not ever have been one. It is also unknown when the gatehouse fell into ruins, leaving it in the decrepit state it is in today. I can only imagine it began its decline during the 1960s.

During the 1970s, the park was virtually in ruins due to vandalism, weather erosion and neglect. In 1972, the first restoration project began with the intentions of returning the park to its former magnificent glory. The park was added to the National Register of Historic Places in 1974. It is also a Registered Yonkers Landmark. The mosaic reflecting pool within the walled garden was restored and refilled with water by 1976. Some people actually used to swim in it.

It was around this time that former member of the Beatles John Lennon visited the park to do a photo shoot for a magazine. The photos were taken by photographer Bob Gruen and are available for viewing on his website www.bobgruen.com.

The lion and unicorn statues in front of the abandoned gatehouse were representations used by several European royal crests.

It was also during these years that a certain group began using the park for its private meetings. For years, there were rumors about a satanic cult performing rituals in the park. The cult called itself the Process Church of the Final Judgment. After investigative reporter Maury Terry wrote his book *The Ultimate Evil*, it seemed the rumors might have been based on truth.

The park became infamous for its midnight black masses by these cultists. The most famous participant of these rituals was the ".44-Caliber Serial Killer," David Berkowitz, aka the "Son of Sam." Berkowitz was a resident of Yonkers at the time. The masses were supposedly held at different locations in the park. Some rumored locations are the Eagle's Nest, the old gatehouse and within a former pump house of the Croton Aqueduct Trail, which became known as the "Devil's Cave." It is also said that animal sacrifices were made. There are even rumors about some young boys being buried in the park.

Sometime around Christmas 1976, two boys found three dead partially mutilated Alsatian or German shepherd dogs lying together in plastic bags along the Old Croton Aqueduct Trail just south of Untermyer Park. The dogs' ears had been carefully removed. The boys buried the animals, believing it was the kind thing to do. However, after the arrest of David Berkowitz on August 10, 1977, the same two boys set out the next day in search of that grave along the Old Croton Aqueduct Trail. Newly aware of Berkowitz's supposed hatred for dogs, the boys believed there could be a connection. Once the grave was discovered, they notified authorities.

During the reign of terror Berkowitz had over New York in the mid-1970s, it seemed there were quite a few dead dogs turning up all over Yonkers. It couldn't be a coincidence, considering his ties to the cult that was known for sacrificing animals—Alsatian dogs in particular.

In November 1979, a Westchester County Police officer unwittingly stumbled on a disturbing night mass at the nearby Lenoir Nature Preserve. He witnessed a group of dark hooded, robed figures carrying torches and leading two leashed Alsatian dogs to their slaughter.

Animal sacrifices have been going on all over the world for thousands of years, usually as a way to appease deities, so it's not too surprising to think it still goes on in today's modern world. Of course, that doesn't mean when dead animals are found in parks, vacant lots or cemeteries that people are not shocked or appalled by it.

One time, while exploring the secrets of Untermyer Park, I found the skeletal remains of a deer. Seeing a dead deer wasn't too surprising, since there are many deer that call the park home. However, it's where the dead deer was found that presents a conundrum.

I was with my wife and teammates at the time. We wanted to take a few photos looking inside an old maintenance room that had been nicknamed "Mr. William's Hole." Supposedly, it earned the name from the cultists, who teased a homeless man named William who frequented the park, saying he lived within the hole in the ground.

We lifted up the metallic door, and I climbed down into this hole to take photos. I was able to stand on a thick concrete wall and took my photos from there. I was hoping to find access to rumored underground tunnels. Instead, there were two small chambers separated by the wall. I could see pipes going across graffiti-covered walls and piles of garbage scattered across the floor. I took my photos and got out.

It wasn't until I checked the photos that I noticed the skeleton of the deer. There is no way a deer could have gotten inside on its own. It would have had to lift the heavy metal door and put it back in place. Someone must have led the deer into the hole and trapped it. It probably starved to death and eventually died.

It looks like whoever was responsible went down afterward and scattered the bones around because they were not together, as they should have been. That's why it was hard to notice at a glance. Of course, there

A rare view looking into a maintenance area known as "Mr. William's Hole." It's in here that I saw the skeletal remains of a deer.

is also a morbid possibility someone could have gone down there and chopped the deer into pieces.

Regardless, my search for these elusive underground tunnels continued. I know for a fact that the Old Croton Aqueduct tunnel passes beneath the western edge of the park. It goes from the Croton Dam upstate all the way down to Manhattan. The trail by the same name runs directly over it, although it's difficult to follow at some points because there are breaks in the trail.

However, there is another tunnel below the park that few people are aware exists. This tunnel goes from the pump room underneath the walled garden and follows under the "1,000 Steps" to the overlook. Directly below the overlook is a secret chamber. According to a person I know of who grew up in Yonkers, there is an altar in this chamber surrounded by stone chairs set in a circle.

Interestingly, Samuel Untermyer was once accused of being a satanist by a British magazine. He was reportedly a member of the Golden Dawn, a fascist political organization that has been known to use Nazi symbolism. Similar symbols can be found on the tiled floor of the pergolas within the walled garden. It is very possible Untermyer used the altar and seats around it for Golden Dawn ceremonies that could have taken place away from prying eyes.

I have spoken to two other people who can confirm this tunnel exists, although I have never been inside it to verify for myself. However, I know I can trust the words of these two individuals since they are both reliable sources. One is a retired police officer whom I used to work with who grew up in Yonkers and saw the tunnel as a teenager. The other was once a security guard at Untermyer Park.

I did, however, see the access point to this tunnel via the pump room. It appears to have been sealed long ago, so exploring it further will most likely never happen.

Mike Matessino, a former resident of Yonkers, recalls walking past the park as a young child. He used to feel a chill whenever he looked at the abandoned carriage house that stood near the park's main entrance on North Broadway. It had been abandoned since 1966.

At one time, the carriage house was going to be renovated and converted into a museum for the park. Unfortunately, in 1983, a devastating fire destroyed it beyond repair. It was demolished in the late 1980s, which was around the same time the mosaic swimming pool was drained (1989). The Charles A. Cola Community Center was built on the site of the carriage house in 1990.

The cryptic designs on these mosaic tiles of the pergola bear resemblances to symbols used by the Golden Dawn.

While the park is quite beautiful by day, it takes on an entirely different tone at night. Some people feel an uneasy sensation of darkness and depression while in certain areas of the park. Strange unexplained images have been known to appear in photographs taken at the park. Disembodied voices are sometimes heard, and numerous EVPs have been captured throughout the park.

A former frequent visitor to the park, John Tantillo told of his past experiences. During the early 1990s, while he was a student at the nearby Mary Elizabeth Seton Junior College, he would sometimes hang out at the park with friends. They preferred to spend their time near the Eagle's Nest Temple of Love gazebo.

One time, while he and his friends were on the stone staircase that passes underneath the Temple of Love, he heard a female child-like voice say either, "Momma" or "Mommy." He claimed there were no children in the area at the time.

When John informed me of this incident, I almost fell off my seat. He had no idea about my Yonkers Ghost Investigators website, nor was he aware of the EVP recordings we've captured at the park. He was genuinely surprised to learn about the two EVP recordings on our website of someone saying,

My wife, Jo-Ann, stops abruptly after hearing a voice saying, "Momma," and then, "Mommy." Our former investigator Amanda, also shown, did not hear the voice.

Both images taken seconds apart show a man walking up from the overlook, but there is a shadow figure behind him in the left image.

"Momma" and then "Mommy," which were both captured during our very first paranormal investigation conducted within the park on October 8, 2011, in the same exact location.

Since that time, we have gotten much more evidence. There was an EVP captured at the old abandoned gatehouse, located along the Carriage Trail, which is not too far from Warburton Avenue. This was our second visit to the gatehouse, and it was at night.

We were inside a small enclosure built into the wall of the hill behind the gatehouse. I believe it may have been used as a cold storage area at one time. During an EVP session inside the room, we captured a female voice asking for help. In that same area, we got a video of a strange light anomaly passing by. Both pieces of evidence are available on our website. Incidentally, this room is sometimes referred to as the "Devil's Hole."

While alone in the walled garden, I was able to record another EVP. I am acquainted with someone named Al. He frequently enjoys going to the garden to feed the fish in the canals, considering he purchased the butterfly koi with his own money and placed them there. Normally, during warm weather, the canals are filled with carp and goldfish. However, during the wintertime, the canals are drained of both fish and water. The fish are given new homes once they are removed.

Conducting an investigation in the Devil's Hole behind the gatehouse. Xavier Gonzalez uses a K2 meter, while I record video. *Photo taken by Jo-Ann Santos-Medina.*

On the afternoon of August 21, 2013, I was sitting on one of the benches along the wall. There was no one else around at the time. I turned on my digital recorder and began an impromptu EVP session. During my line of questioning, I asked the name of the person who likes to feed the fish in the garden. Before I could finish my question, a female voice answered, "Al."

I got excited when I later listened to my recording and heard the response. It was further proof the park is haunted by intelligent spirits who can actually communicate.

After the tragic events of September 11, 2001, when terrorists destroyed the World Trade Center in New York City, a memorial was established for the fallen heroes of that day and fallen firefighters and police officers of Yonkers' past. The memorial is located near the entrance of the park across from the parking lot.

Today, efforts are constantly being made to beautify the park. Boy Scouts and workers from the Yonkers Department of Parks, Recreation and Conservation have helped to clean up debris and excavate artifacts. In April 2014, the Boy Scouts Troop 5 of Bronxville cleared out the area around the gatehouse. The Untermyer Gardens Conservancy has by far played the biggest role in restoring the park's monuments, statues, gardens and grounds. Untermyer Park is slowly beginning to reclaim its once wondrous beauty.

During the summertime, the Untermyer Performing Arts Council (UPAC), which was established in 1976, holds free concerts in the park on Saturday evenings from around 7:00 p.m. to 9:30 p.m. The concerts are held on the summer stage in front of the walled garden beginning the last Saturday of June and ending on the first Saturday of September.

In May 2015, an iron fence was erected going from the walled garden to behind the summer stage and south along the Carriage Trail to the gate near the playground of the Richmond Center. The purpose of the fence is to prevent trespassers from exploring the park at night and to keep deer from disturbing the performances on the stage. Many visitors were against the idea because it takes away from the beauty and makes it look as if you are on the outside looking in.

The office for the Untermyer Performing Arts Council is located within the Charles A. Cola Community Center near the entrance of the park. Office hours are from 9:00 a.m. to 3:00 p.m.

The Richmond Center is now a place that cares for the mentally disabled. During the summer of 2014, while I was attending one of the free concerts, a female nurse who works the nightshift informed me that she believes the facility is haunted. While she did not really elaborate, she simply claimed the place gives her the creeps. Numerous patients have died there over the years, so the possibility for a haunting is high, but I seriously doubt I will ever be allowed to do a paranormal investigation at an active healthcare facility.

In my opinion, based on the stories I've heard, the park's history, my personal experiences and the paranormal investigations conducted by my team, Untermyer Park is by far the most haunted location in Yonkers. It is fitting for it to be the last Yonkers location mentioned in this book because I literally saved the best for last.

Van Cortlandt Park

And now for a bonus location that is no longer in the city of Yonkers, although it used to be.

I can remember passing Van Cortlandt Park many times in my life, first by bus or taxi and then years later in my own car. I've been to the 1,146-acre park on many occasions. It's one of the finest and largest parks in New York City. It also helps to mark the border between the Bronx and Yonkers.

Up until 1873, the park used to be part of Westchester County and was once referred to as Lower Yonkers, together with the area of Mile Square. In fact, most of the Bronx once belonged to Westchester County, as the town of Kingsbridge on the west and the borough of Westchester to the east. Below that was Morrisania. This changed when the two previous areas mentioned seceded from Westchester County to join a few other regions in the formation of the Bronx in 1874, when it was added as a borough of New York City. This is my main reason for including this park in a book about Yonkers.

Once part of the Van Cortlandt estate, this park still has a few interesting links to its past that are often overlooked by its hundreds of daily visitors. The former Frederick Van Cortlandt House still stands and is now the Van Cortlandt House Museum. It is located within the park and can be seen from Broadway at around West 246 Street. Built using rough stone from 1748 to 1749, it is the oldest house in the Bronx.

During the American Revolutionary War, General George Washington stayed at the house in 1776, 1781 and on November 18, 1783, using it as one of his many temporary headquarters. Within the house, there is a room that is referred to as the Washington Room, which is one of the finer rooms of the museum.

Van Cortland House during the early 1900s. *Courtesy of the Yonkers Historical Society.*

On the early morning of August 31, 1778, during the Battle of Kingsbridge, also called the Battle of Tibbetts Brook, British lieutenant colonel John Graves Simcoe marched his five hundred men from Kingsbridge into the woods, where he'd soon divide his troops and surround his enemy. During the battle, Native Americans from Stockbridge to the north came to the aid of the Continental army. Chief Daniel Nimham and his son, Captain Abraham Nimham, led about forty battle-hardened warriors into the very same woods, where they'd eventually meet up with the British.

As it turned out, the Native warriors were greatly outnumbered, and they were quickly surrounded by their enemy in the old Van Cortlandt Woods, which are now a part of the park in the Woodlawn Heights section. They put up a good fight, but they lacked the proper weapons to contend with their more advanced enemy. Chief Nimham was able to wound Lieutenant Colonel Simcoe, but soon afterward, the chief fell at the hands of a Hussar, a type of Hungarian light cavalryman. Many of the Natives were either killed or injured, including Chief Nimham and his son. Their scattered bodies were left as carrion for the wild dogs and crows to feed upon.

Chief Nimham was the last sachem (chief) of the Wappinger people. He and his son, along with sixteen other warriors, were buried where they fell in an area now known as Indian Field. Nothing says haunted like an ancient Indian burial ground. It is said the chief still haunts the field today. I would imagine he's not too pleased. The field is located between Jerome Avenue and Van Cortlandt Park Avenue East starting at East 233 Street across from Woodlawn Cemetery in the Bronx and continues north from there.

On June 14, 1906, a memorial plaque was placed on a stone in the park at Oneida Avenue near East 238 Street. The Bronx Chapter of the Daughters of the American Revolution dedicated it in memory of the chief and his fellow fallen warriors, who gave all to help this country gain its independence.

The name for Oneida Avenue comes from the Oneida Nation, which many of the remaining Stockbridge natives joined by the 1800s. Farther north in the town of Kent, Putnam County, Nimham Mountain was named after the chief.

During a visit in the early part of 2015, I noticed someone had left two folded American flags in honor of the fallen warriors. Hopefully, they remain there for a long time to come as a testament to these brave souls. It's ironic how these selfless warriors would someday sacrifice their lives to help the colonists gain their independence when it was only about one hundred years earlier that the colonists had practically chased their tribes away, causing them to migrate north in the first place.

This is not the only burial ground located in the park. There are two others. Far across the parade ground field opposite from the Van Cortlandt House Museum is a hill. If you follow a path around the back of the hill closer to the golf course, you will reach a second path that leads up the hill to an old walled cemetery. The cemetery is surrounded by trees and partially hidden by a fairly high wall that goes around three sides of it. An old iron fence blocks the fourth side, which faces east leading to the path, where the entrance gate is located. It is locked with a chain and padlock. The pillars at either side of the gate are missing the top decorative pieces that once adorned them. A small Parks Department sign on the fence to the right side of the entrance gate indicates the name of the hill in white lettering over the leaf that is the Park Department's logo. It simply reads, "Vault Hill."

Supposedly, during the American Revolutionary War, the Continental army hid New York City records within the vaults of this hill, after the Battle of Long Island. When the British became aware of the records' location, the records were hastily removed and hidden elsewhere in the city.

Later in the war, before General George Washington set out for Yorktown, Virginia, he left several fires burning atop Vault Hill to act as a distraction. His plan was to fool the British into thinking the Continental army was still

This page: The Indian Field Memorial dedicated to Chief Daniel Nimham and the brave warriors who fell in battle on the morning of August 31, 1778.

in Lower Yonkers. The plan was a success. The fires were kept burning for several days, until Washington's men could move across the Hudson River and make their way south through New Jersey. Washington's troops were well on their way to Yorktown by the time British general Sir Henry Clinton discovered the clever ruse.

At one time, there were multiple gravestones marking the graves of Van Cortlandt family members on Vault Hill. However, over the decades, they were knocked over and destroyed by vandals. Drug addicts would often sneak into the cemetery to get high, since it was a place where they could not be seen. My good friend and fellow team member Rich Embree can recall visiting the park when he was a kid and seeing the gate to the cemetery, which was open back then, and the gravestones that had been deliberately knocked over.

On a visit during December 29, 2014, I could only count two tombstones at Vault Hill. Both are badly damaged, and there are no names visible to indicate who is buried there, aside from the inscription on the steps leading to the gate. It identifies the location as the "Burial Plot of the Van Cortlandt Family."

The third burial ground in the park belonged to the Tibbetts family. In 1732, Jacobus Van Cortlandt purchased the land from George Tibbetts, who stipulated that a family cemetery included on the land be reserved for future

An early 1900s overhead shot of Vault Hill looking toward the Van Cortlandt Lake. *Courtesy of the Yonkers Historical Society.*

Looking into the Van Cortlandt family burial ground during the early 1900s. *Courtesy of the Yonkers Historical Society.*

generations of the Tibbetts family. Tibbetts had made the same agreement in 1717 when he acquired the land from the Betts family. The cemetery had become the burial ground for both the Betts and Tibbetts families for many generations, dating back as far as 1668.

Over the years, this cemetery has had several names. It has been called the Tibbetts Family Cemetery, the Berrian-Bashford Burying Ground and, in later years, the Kingsbridge Burial Ground.

In 1888, the Van Cortlandt family sold the grounds, along with the house and burying grounds, to New York City for use as a public park. The majority of the remaining grain fields were converted into the current parade grounds, walking pathways were built and the house became a museum.

During the 1880s, a local historian by the name of Thomas H. Edsall visited the old Kingsbridge Burial Ground and noticed that most of the graves were marked by fieldstones containing little or no inscriptions. The few stones that had inscriptions mainly had the initials of the deceased on them, although five did have dates. The dates ranged from 1794 to 1808 and belonged to the graves of Ackerman, Berrian and Bashford family members, who were descended from the Betts and Tibbetts families.

These gravestones are long gone now. In many ways, the cemetery is long gone, as well. Nothing remains of the Kingsbridge Burial Ground, aside

This photo from 2014 shows the burial ground on Vault Hill today.

The Kingsbridge Burial Ground looking toward the Van Cortlandt Lake during the early 1900s. *Courtesy of the Yonkers Historical Society.*

from the ancient remains buried deep underground. It used to be located to the lower left side of the Van Cortlandt Lake, surrounded by a short iron pipe fence, which is still there today. It marks the edge of the walking path. Unfortunately, the gravestones fell victim to vandalism and weather erosion long ago. Combined with the overgrowth of greenery around it, the location of this lost cemetery is barely recognizable anymore.

In 1902, an old prison window from the Rhinelander Sugar House at Duane and Rose Streets in lower Manhattan was moved to the rear of the Van Cortlandt House, after the sugarhouse was demolished in 1892. During the American Revolutionary War, the British used many of the sugarhouses as makeshift prisons. An iron fence currently surrounds it. Considering how many prisoners died in custody, it leaves one to wonder if that prison window brought along a few ghosts of its own.

Not too far away on the other side of the Van Cortlandt Lake is the oldest existing public golf course in the country. When the Van Cortlandt Park Golf Course opened in 1895, it only had nine holes, as opposed to the current eighteen holes spanning the course. At one time, Moe, Larry and Curly, the original Three Stooges, maintained lockers at the golf club.

This old arched brick prison window from the Rhinelander Sugar House in Manhattan was placed in a fenced area behind the Van Cortlandt House in 1902, after the sugarhouse was demolished.

Incidentally, the Van Cortlandt Lake is the largest freshwater lake in New York City.

Nearby, just south from the lake across from the Van Cortlandt Golf House are the metallic skeletal remnants of an old New York Putnam Railroad station, whose rusted ruins now stand along the path of the South County Trail. On either side of the ruins are old iron bridges, where trains used to cross. On either side of each bridge lie a few half buried wooden tracks that can barely be seen on the ground along the trail.

If you follow the trail heading north, you will come across a strange sight. There is a long line of stone pillars resembling some sort of modern-day Stonehenge hidden away between the lake and parade grounds, although these stone pillars cannot be seen from the parade grounds due to the dense trees.

Regardless of how odd they may seem, there really is no big mystery involved here. These thirteen stone pillars were built during the 1910s as a way of sampling different types of stone to test their durability for the construction of Grand Central Station in Manhattan. In the end, the New York Central Railroad chose Indiana limestone, from which the two pillars at the far north are made. The pillars have since been painted over to cover the graffiti that once marred their surface.

These stone monoliths are affectionately known as the Stonehenge of Van Cortlandt Park. They are beyond the Parade Grounds parallel to the South County Trail.

Another trail that goes through the park is the Old Croton Aqueduct Trail, which was built directly over the old aqueduct tunnels. The tunnels go from the Croton River upstate all the way down to New York City, where it once supplied water to the metropolis from the mid-1800s until the mid-1900s. Now the tunnels are abandoned and have been sealed off. However, along this vast trail one can still find small ventilation towers and old pump houses. The trail runs parallel to the South County Trail, although it is on the east side of the golf course.

In July 1916, Squadron A of New York State's mounted troops gathered at the parade grounds of the park, where they set up a temporary camp. They had assembled for a gala sendoff to Mexico, where they were to hunt down notorious Mexican rebel leader Pancho Villa. They would not succeed.

Farther north, there is a twenty-one-acre horse ranch called the Riverdale Equestrian Centre, located in the park at around West 254 Street and Broadway. Visitors are allowed the opportunity to ride horses. When I was a young boy, my cousin and I once rode ponies there. It was a fun experience for us, although it didn't smell very good. Still, it was a small price to pay for a great memory that I will cherish for the rest of my life. Unfortunately, the ranch no longer allows "drop-in" horse and pony rides. However, it does offer private and group riding lessons to children and adults at a cost, as well as an after-school program.

The Van Cortlandt House was added to the National Register of Historic Places in 1967. It became a historic landmark in 1976. A public swimming pool was added in 1970. On April 14, 1998, a Canine Court was established, where people could take their dogs, thanks to Parks Commissioner Henry Stern.

There is no doubt that Van Cortlandt Park has a great many wonders to behold, but it also has its dark secrets and legends. There have been documented cases of both suicides and murders committed in the park. One story I used to hear about when I was a kid visiting my family in Yonkers was about several heads that had been found in the rear of Van Cortlandt Park near the border of Yonkers. The heads supposedly belonged to young boys or teenagers.

I have searched for any tangible proof or documentation to back up this story and have repeatedly come up empty. I often wonder if there was ever any truth to it. Perhaps it was a story told to keep young kids from venturing too deep into the park without supervision, especially since the only people I heard the story from were adults who had children who liked to play near the park.

From where my cousin lived at the end of Caryl Avenue, there was an opening into the park at a dead end street, which had a path that eventually leads to Broadway. However, first you'd have to walk through the park for a few minutes surrounded by woods. Naturally, it's not the kind of path a parent wants his or her child to walk through alone. I am pretty sure there have been plenty of robberies committed along this path, as well as on some of the other paths. Therefore, I can understand the need to make up stories that would scare kids away from daring to follow this isolated path.

Today, there is a fence covering the bulk of this particular park entrance, but there is still an opening at the end that leads to the path. It just isn't as wide open or easily visible as it was when I was younger.

One similar story that does have truth to it was about a pair of legs found near the Tibbetts Wetlands of the park. On the evening of November 22, 1921, a woman's legs were discovered near a puddle of water by a man on his way home from work. The legs had been severed from the body just above the knees and were still wearing black stockings. There was also a newspaper with the legs dated October 20, 1921. Several pieces of brown twine had been used to bind the legs together.

The legs were believed to belong to the torso of a woman found near Queens Boulevard and Rawson Street in Long Island City a month earlier on October 22. However, the legs only showed slight signs of decomposition, which meant they had somehow been preserved. The legs were taken to the city morgue for comparison. Both the chief medical examiner and the captain of the Homicide Bureau of New York City believed they belonged to the same victim.

In July 1923, the Ku Klux Klan burned a five-foot cross around East 213 Street near Jerome Avenue in the park as a warning against the mingling of Caucasians and African Americans in the Bronx. It was the first time the Klan had ever dared to leave its signature mark in the borough of the Bronx. The burning cross was later knocked over by a New York City bicycle police officer named McGrath.

Van Cortlandt Park is owned by the New York City Department of Parks and Recreation, and the Van Cortlandt Park Conservancy maintains it regularly. The park is conveniently located between two New York City elevated train lines, the number 1 train on Broadway and the number 4 train on Jerome Avenue.

CONCLUSION

M ost of the locations featured in this book are still standing today. Only a few are long gone. Of course, the residential locations are all privately owned, and therefore I could not provide their exact addresses. On the other hand, most of the non-residential locations are places that can be visited. Some are even friendly to the idea of paranormal investigations being conducted. All one needs to do is ask. I don't guarantee you will experience anything paranormal after one visit. Sometimes it takes several visits before any evidence can be collected.

I am grateful to have been given the opportunity to research these fascinating locations. I tried to provide as much historical information as possible while also telling the paranormal stories of each location. In some cases, I was unable to verify certain events, and for that, I apologize. It was not without effort. There are simply things that cannot be verified. Often it might be because they never took place. That's the thing with urban legends. You can't always prove them right or wrong.

The Yonkers Historical Society has played a vital role in preserving the history of Yonkers, as well as with the designation of landmarks and the protection of parks and historic sites such as Philipse Manor Hall. It has also pushed to make the old less-favored sites, such as Boyce Thompson Institute, into historic landmarks. Their efforts helped to save Boyce Thompson Institute from almost certain demolition in 2014. Plans are already underway to renovate the building.

I've also heard that renovations of the Glenwood Power Plant have been delayed, most likely due to financial reasons. Hopefully, work will resume soon. I would like to see what becomes of that place.

While this book might already be published, it doesn't mean I'm not searching for additional information regarding the locations featured here, as well as other places that might be haunted. If you have any useful information you can provide that would help add credibility or debunk any of the hauntings mentioned in this book, please contact me. My e-mail address is Ginvestigators@aol.com.

I continue to conduct paranormal investigations with my team at different locations both in and outside of Yonkers. We are always looking for new places to investigate. If you believe your home is haunted and would like someone to check it out for you, we can do so free of charge. We do it because we enjoy it. Naturally, we can keep your situation private, if that's what you'd prefer.

If you wish to contact us with regard to an investigation, please e-mail me, find us on *Facebook* or refer to our website, www.YonkersGhostInvestigators.com.

BIBLIOGRAPHY

"Abraham Lincoln's Letter to Yonkers." *Yonkers Historical Society Newsletter* 5, no. 1 (Spring 1996).

Alemzadeh, Laura. "Keeping New York Moving for a Quarter Century." *Yonkers Historian* 22, no. 3 (Fall 2013).

"Animated by Reverence for the Past." *Yonkers Historical Bulletin* 13, no. 1 (January 1966).

Armour, R.C. *North American Indian Fairy Tales, Folklore and Legends.* Philadelphia: Gibbings and Company, 1905.

Atkins, Thomas Astley. *Indian Wars and the Uprising of 1655—Yonkers Depopulated. A Paper Read Before the Yonkers Historical and Library Association, Etc.* New York: British Library, the Society, 1892.

———. *The Manor of Philipsburg: A Paper Read Before the New York Historical Society.* New Delhi, India: Isha Books, 2004.

Benjamin, Vernon. *The History of the Hudson River Valley from Wilderness to the Civil War.* New York: Overlook Press, 2014.

Bliven, Emma. "The Day General Washington Came to Yonkers." *Yonkers Historical Bulletin* 17, no. 2 (July 1970).

Brown, Henry Collins. "Washington Meets Mary Philipse." *Old Yonkers—1646–1922: A Page of History.* Reprinted in "About Yonkers History, Part IV." *Quarterly Journal of the Yonkers Historical Society: Yonkers History* 7, no. 3 (Fall 1998).

Dacquinto, Vincent T. *Hauntings of the Hudson River Valley: An Investigative Journey.* Charleston, SC: The History Press, 2007.

D'Agnillo, John. "William Boyce Thompson: An Enduring Legacy in Yonkers." *Quarterly Journal of the Yonkers Historical Society: Yonkers History* 8, no. 2 (Summer 1999).

Dawson, Henry Barton. *Papers Concerning the Town and Village of Yonkers, Westchester County: A Fragment.* Yonkers, NY: Nabu Press, 1866.

Department of Publicity of the Yonkers Board of Trade. *Yonkers Illustrated.* Salem, MA: Higginson Book Company, 2007.

Dickson, Isabelle Cornell. "Thomas C. Cornell, 1819–1894." *Yonkers Historical Bulletin* 14, no. 2 (July 1967).

Dunwell, Frances F. *The Hudson: America's River.* New York: Columbia University Press, 2008.

Friends of Philipse Manor Hall. *Philipse Manor Hall State Historic Guide.* Yonkers, NY: self-published, n.d.

Gethard, Chris. *Weird New York.* New York: Sterling Publishing Co., 2005.

Hansen, Kris A. *Death Passage on the Hudson: The Wreck of the Henry Clay.* New York: Purple Mountain Press, 2004.

Harper, Helen Leale. "Dr. Charles A. Leale, First Surgeon to Reach the Assassinated President Abraham Lincoln." *Yonkers Historical Society Newsletter*, Spring 1995.

Hauck, Dennis William. *Haunted Places: The National Directory.* New York: Penguin Group, 1994.

Hoar, Mary. "On This Day in Yonkers History…" *Yonkers Rising* 109, no. 43 (October 24, 2014).

———. "The Enchanted Gardens of Greystone." *Yonkers Historian* 19, no. 1 (Spring 2010).

Irving, Washington. *Knickerbocker's History of New York*. New York: Putnam, 1824.

Jennings, Joan, and Luis Perelman. *Images of America: Yonkers*. Charleston, SC: Arcadia Publishing, 2013.

John, F. Wallace. "The Building of Manor Hall." *Yonkers Historical Bulletin* 10, no. 2 (December 1963).

John, F.W. "The Austin Pickle Farm on the Saw Mill River." *Yonkers Historical Bulletin* 13, no. 1 (January 1966).

———. "The Saving of Manor Hall." *Yonkers Historical Bulletin* 14, no. 1 (January 1967).

———. "The Yonkers Chapter of the Westchester Historical Society." *Yonkers Historical Bulletin* 14, no. 2 (July 1967).

Kruk, Jonathan. *Legends and Lore of Sleepy Hollow and the Hudson Valley*. Charleston, SC: The History Press, 2011.

"Landmarks Committee Announces Six More Designations." *Yonkers Historical Bulletin* 15, no. 2 (July 1968).

Leslie, Frank. "Mr. Tilden at Greystone." *Frank Leslies' Illustrated Newspaper*, July 5, 1884. Reprinted, *Yonkers Historian* 13, no. 2 (Summer 2004).

Lewis, Tom. *The Hudson: A History*. New Haven, CT: Yale University Press, 2005.

Macken, Lynda Lee. *Haunted Houses of the Hudson Valley*. Ann Arbor, MI: Sheridan Books, 2006.

McCadden, Helen M. "Life in Yonkers a Century Ago—In 1872, When Yonkers Became a City." *Yonkers Historical Bulletin* 19, no. 2 (Summer 1972).

Newtown, Michael. *The Encyclopedia of Serial Killers*. 2nd ed. New York: Facts on File, Inc., an imprint of Infobase Publishing, 2000.

New York Evening Telegram. "Klan Displays Fiery Cross in N.Y. City Park," July 12, 1923.

New York Sun. "New York in Pictures, No. 88: Van Cortlandt Family Cemetery," October 21, 1927.

New York Times. "Shark or Sea Serpent," June 9, 1899.

Panetta, Roger, in conjunction with the Hudson River Museum. *Westchester: The American Suburb*. New York: Fordham University Press, 2006.

Parish-Bischoff, Donna. *The Lee Avenue Haunting*. New York: DPB Publishing, 2013.

"Plaques Unveiled at Untermyer Park." *Yonkers Historical Bulletin* 21, no. 2 (Summer 1974).

Portion of City of Yonkers and Westchester County Map. New York: Watson and Company, 1891.

Queens (NY) Daily Star. "Girl's Legs Found in Bronx Declared to be Those of L.I. City Murder Victim," November 23, 1921.

Rinaldi, Thomas E., and Robert J. Yasinsac. *Hudson Valley Ruins: Forgotten Landmarks of an American Landscape*. Lebanon, NH: University Press of New England, 2006.

Sarchie, Ralph, and Lisa Collier Cool. *Beware the Night*. New York: St. Martin's Press, 2001.

Scharf, J. Thomas. *History of Westchester County*. Vol. 2. Philadelphia: L.E. Preston and Company, 1886.

Shelley, Thomas J. *Dunwoodie: The History of St. Joseph's Seminary, Yonkers, New York*. Westminster, MD: Christian Classics, Inc., 1993.

Simpson, Jeffrey. *The Hudson River, 1850–1918: A Photographic Portrait*. Tarrytown, NY: Sleepy Hollow Press, 1981.

Swanson, Susan Cochran, and Elizabeth Green Fuller, in conjunction with the Westchester County Historical Society. *Westchester County: A Pictorial History (Revised Edition)*. Virginia Beach, VA: Donning Company, 1982.

"Telegram for Mr. Prime!" (The City Centennial—Historic Scene When Yonkers Became a City is Reenacted at City Hall). *Yonkers Historical Bulletin* 29, no. 2 (Summer 1972).

Terry, Maury. *The Ultimate Evil: The Truth About the Cult Murders: Son of Sam & Beyond*. New York: Barnes & Noble Digital, 2001.

Tompkins, Louise. "The Mighty Hudson." *Pine Plains (NY) Register Herald*, June 16–17, 1982.

Twomey, Bill, and Thomas X. Casey. *Images of America: Northwest Bronx*. Charleston, SC: Arcadia Publishing, 2011.

"A Visit to Yonkers, 1857" by Neutral Tint. Originally Published in *Ballou's Pictorial Drawing-Room Companion*, March 27, 1857, Modified by the Yonkers Historical Society, *Yonkers Historian* 12, no. 3 (Fall 2003).

Walton, Frank L. *Pillars of Yonkers*. New York: Stratford House, 1951.

Weigold, Marilyn E., and the Yonkers Historical Society. *Yonkers in the Twentieth Century*. Albany: State University of New York Press, 2014.

Westchester County Department of Parks, Recreation and Conservation. *A Guide to the Westchester County Department of Parks, Recreation & Conservation*. Westchester County, NY: self-published, 2002.

Westchester Weekend. "Refurbished Philipse Manor Opens," July 16, 1976.

"Yonkers Becomes a City." *Quarterly Journal of the Yonkers Historical Society: Yonkers History* 7, no. 3 (Fall 1998).

Yonkers Historical Bulletin: Some Reminiscences of the Old Philipse Manor House in Yonkers and Its Surroundings 34, no. 1 (1988–89).

Yonkers Historical Calendar 2005. Yonkers, NY: Yonkers Historical Society Publications Committee, 2005.

Yonkers Historical Society and the Blue Door Artist Association. *Then and Now: Yonkers*. Charleston, SC: Arcadia Publishing, 2008.

Yonkers (NY) Herald Statesman. "Copcutt Mansion Spawned Many a Spooky Tale." July 18, 1972.

Yonkers, N.Y., Map. New York: Landis and Hughes, 1899.

Yonkers (NY) Statesman and News. "Woodlawn a Historic Spot: Scene of Revolution Battles," January 24, 1924.

WEBSITE SOURCES

http://abandonednyc.com/2012/08/28/knocking-at-the-gates-of-hell-in-yonkers/ (Glenwood Power Plant)

http://american-buddha.com/cult.unholyalliance.2.9.htm (Untermyer Park)

http://www.americanrevolutionarywar.net/

http://antimatrix.org/Convert/Books/Andrew.Carrington.Hitchcock/Synagogue. of.Satan/1878-1919.htm#Woodrow_Wilson_blackmailed (Untermyer Park)

http://www.bedofnailz.com/buckout.html (Information related to Oakland Cemetery)

www.bobgruen.com (Untermyer Park)

http://collections.westchestergov.com/cdm/search/collection/pjg!pmc!ppc!pls!ppl!pcs/order/title/page/30/display/200 (Misc. Yonkers history)

http://davidberkowitz.wikispaces.com/Capture+and+Sentencing

http://dmna.ny.gov/a_history/rev-war.html (Information regarding the American Revolutionary War)

http://www.encyclopedia.com/topic/Hudson_River.aspx

http://www.examiner.com/article/ghosts-yank-bed-sheets-yonkers (Walnut Street Boarding House)

https://www.facebook.com/ (Various groups related to Yonkers)

http://www.fs.cornell.edu/fs/facinfo/fs_facilInfo.cfm?facil_cd=1076 (Boyce Thompson Institute)

http://www.fultonhistory.com/Fulton.html (Numerous newspaper articles)

http://www.ghostshipsoftheworld.com/2013/10/ghostly-storm-ship-of-hudson-river-new.html

http://www.ghostsofamerica.com/1/New_York_Yonkers_ghost_sightings.html

http://gnadenhutten.tripod.com/patriotsblood/id4.html (Van Cortlandt Park)

http://www.governor.ny.gov/news/governor-cuomo-announces-start-construction-27-million-affordable-housing-complex-yonkers (Public School 6) http://www.gutenberg.org/files/27701/27701-h/27701-h.htm (Misc. Yonkers history)

http://www.history.com/news/ask-history/were-witches-burned-at-the-stake-during-the-salem-witch-trials

http://www.hudsonvalleyruins.org (Glenwood Power Plant and Public School 6)

http://www.loc.gov/pictures/ (Misc. photos relating to Yonkers history)

http://www.mywedding.com/baddleycitron/custom3.html - My Wedding (Alder Manor)

http://news.hamlethub.com/swyonkers/life/836-animal-sacrifice-in-westchester

https://nycemetery.wordpress.com/2011/05/18/kingsbridge-burial-ground/

http://www.nycgovparks.org/parks/VanCortlandtPark/highlights/11610

http://nyc.mommypoppins.com/newyorkcitykids/horseback-riding-nyc-kids-lessons-pony-rides (Van Cortlandt Park)

http://www.nysac.org/counties/westchester-county-history.php (Misc. Westchester County history)

http://nysparks.com (Information on several parks and trails)

http://www.peachridgeglass.com/2012/08/blue-wells-miller-provost-blue-cathedral-pepper-sauce-question/ (St. Joseph's Cemetery historical connection)

http://philipsemanorhall.blogspot.com/p/blog-page.html

http://politicalgraveyard.com/geo/NY/ofc/yonkers.html (Yonkers historical information)

http://quadupdates.blogspot.com/2008/11/hudson-river-monster-returns.html

http://www.rootsweb.ancestry.com/~nywestch/history/index.htm (Misc. Westchester County history)

http://www.rootsweb.ancestry.com/~nywestch/manors/philipse1.htm

http://www.scoutingny.com/the-abandoned-boyce-thompson-institute/

http://www.sonofsamconspiracy.com/

http://theplant.com/overview/ (Glenwood Power Plant)

http://theshadowlands.net/ghost/

http://untappedcities.com/2013/11/07/daily-what-13-stone-pillars-van-cortlandt-park-tests-grand-central-terminal-facade/

http://victoriansource.com (Misc. information related to Philipse Manor Hall and Untermyer Park)

http://weatherdork.weebly.com/educational-blogs/the-ghost-ship-of-the-hudson-river

http://www.westchesterhistory.com/ (Misc. Westchester County history)

http://en.wikipedia.org/wiki/Main_Page (Numerous historic figures, photos, locations, and other information related to Yonkers history)

http://www.yonkerschamber.com/history.html (Yonkers historical information)

http://yonkers.dailyvoice.com/news/yonkers-iconic-power-plant-readies-facelift (Glenwood Power Plant)

http://www.yonkersghostinvestigators.com/haunted-locations.html

http://www.yonkershistory.org/joucode.html (Yonkers historical information)

http://www.yonkersny.gov/ (Misc. facts about Yonkers)

https://www.youtube.com (The Putnam Division Yesterday and Today, Son of Sam Speaks, and Serial Killers—David Berkowitz [Son of Sam]—Documentary)

http://www.ypl.org/localnewspapers (Information regarding Yonkers newspapers)

ABOUT THE AUTHOR

Jason Medina at Untermyer Park near the Eagle's Nest in December 2013. *Photo taken by Jo-Ann Santos-Medina.*

Born and raised in the Bronx, New York, Jason Medina lived there until his late twenties. While growing up, he'd often write his own comic books or make up stories. In the third grade, he won an award for a book-making contest.

However, it wasn't until moving to Yonkers that he'd consider the possibility of turning one of his stories into a book. He found himself going through his old stories and immediately found one that would be perfect to turn into a novel. It was a fictional story he'd written in 1990 called *The Diary of Audrey Malone Frayer*, although the story required some tweaking before it was ready.

In 2006, Jason picked up a new hobby. Together with his cousins, he formed the Yonkers Ghost Investigators. They began going to locations within Yonkers that were rumored to be haunted. It didn't hurt that he lived near three cemeteries.

In time, a website was created for his team as a way to show off the evidence collected during the group's paranormal investigations. There are currently hundreds of photos, numerous videos and many EVP sound bites on the website.

His interest in the paranormal led him on a new path, but it didn't take long for him to come up with a new idea for a book. This would become his first published novel. While investigating haunted locations, he learned about an abandoned psychiatric hospital on Long Island in a village called Kings Park. After seeing the place in person, he had no doubt it would make a great setting for quite a few stories.

In 2008, he began writing a manuscript titled "A Forgotten Man in a Forgotten Land," which takes place at the Kings Park Psychiatric Center. Soon he decided to create two additional short stories about two of the supporting characters in order to provide a better background for them. These extra stories prompted him to rename the book to a more appropriate title suitable for each character. Thus, *No Hope for the Hopeless at Kings Park* was born. The book was completed and published in the summer of 2013.

It was a proud moment for the new author, but there was little time to stop and smell the roses. He was on the verge of retirement from his twenty-three-year career with the New York City Police Department and wanted to have his next book ready before his retirement was official.

During his research of the abandoned psychiatric hospital, he got the idea to begin work on a historical account of the hospital. He already had enough research material to write out a hefty-sized documentary-style book that would include maps, photos of the past and present, as well as stories from former patients and employees. This book would be called *Kings Park Psychiatric Center: A Journey Through History*.

Naturally, a project of this magnitude would require great care in getting the facts right. It could not be rushed. His research would have to be more extensive, and he'd need to interview more people. To make things more difficult, recent demolitions of some buildings caused an unexpected delay.

In the meantime, he worked on his story *The Diary of Audrey Malone Frayer* and improved it. He put his heart and soul into each character, allowing them to come to life for the reader. The book was published in March 2014, completing his goal. His retirement would not be official until a month later, and he already had two books published.

In 2013, a representative from The History Press contacted Jason. She had come across his websites and decided he would be a good choice to write a book about haunted locations in Yonkers. Of course, he was deeply honored but totally swamped with work, the upcoming publication of his first book at the time and his other projects.

Fortunately, the people at The History Press understood his obligations and waited patiently for the right time. After the publication of his second book, Jason contacted them to let them know he was ready. Within a month, a contract was signed and he began working on *Ghosts and Legends of Yonkers*.

Ghosts and Legends of Yonkers is Jason's first real chance at historical nonfiction, but it will not be his last. Keep an eye out for *KPPC: A Journey Through History*, which will be the definitive history of the abandoned Kings Park Psychiatric Center. Expect it to be released before the end of 2015. In addition, another fictional novel entitled *A Ghost in New Orleans* should also be published by the time you read this book. For more information on these books and his other future projects, please refer to his personal website, www.JasonMedinaTribalPublications.com.